CW01431015

LIBER NOCTIS

A HANDBOOK OF THE SORCEROUS ARTE

Gary St. M. Nottingham

PUBLISHED BY AVALONIA

www.avaloniabooks.co.uk

Published by Avalonia

BM Avalonia
London
WC1N 3XX
England, UK
www.avaloniabooks.co.uk

LIBER NOCTIS
Copyright Gary St. Michael Nottingham 2004

First Edition 2004.
This revised edition, 2015.

All rights reserved.

ISBN 978-1-905297-74-0

Design by Satori, for Avalonia.

British Library Cataloguing in Publication Data. A catalogue record for this book is available from the British Library.

LIBER NOCTIS

FOUNDATIONS OF PRACTICAL SORCERY VOLUME I

About the Author

Gary St. M. Nottingham's commitment to the study and practice of the alchemical arte, ritual magic, grimoires and spirit conjuration means that he can often be found peering at bubbling flasks or a shewstone – or otherwise engaged in deepening his knowledge and understanding of such matters. His practices also draw on the work of the 17th-century astrologer William Lilly and the arte of horary astrology.

Gary was raised in south Shropshire, where, during his mid-teens, he became involved with a small Coven, thereby gaining an excellent grounding in a wide selection of magical practices. Following the conjuration of a spirit, and asking it for help that manifested when least expected, he subsequently became involved with a group of practising alchemists. He has a background in horticulture, enjoys spending time in the garden and playing chess. He organised the legendary Ludlow Esoteric Conference (2004-2008), helped produce *Verdelet* occult magazine, has taught many free day workshops on basic occult skills and is a popular speaker at esoteric conferences.

The seven volumes of *Foundations of Practical Sorcery* are an unabridged collection of Gary's much sought-after previously published work, updated and made available to a wider readership at last.

Dedicated to RB

'Mistress of that Arte'

Table of Contents

Introduction

We live in an age where we are awash with information on all subjects, and to this the magical artes are no exception. Whilst the student of magic can easily access all manner of electronic files there is nothing quite like a book.

A book can not only be picked up and read, but will, in many instances, over time, become a friend, guide and teacher who has assisted the reader on their journey throughout their life. Quite simply books can change lives and this is why those who have been in positions of power through the centuries have tried, and often failed, to keep knowledge out of the hands of everyday folk. This is perhaps primarily because they feared the power of the book to cause change, and change is what the seven books in the Foundations of Practical Sorcery series will cause.

Today the magical artes have never been so accessible, although that doesn't mean the demands that the arte makes upon the practitioner have been lessened in any way. While the arte is, in principle, for all, not everyone will have the self-discipline, the will and the imagination to succeed therein. However for those who do have these basic attributes or are prepared to acquire them there is much to be gained from the practice of magic in all levels of life. For many people their ingress into the arte will be by books, and the exploration of and working with the information they contain. There is nothing like experience even if your magic proves less successful than hoped for: there is no such thing as failure in magic, because every experience will, at the very least, teach the practitioner something, even if it's just to try harder next time!

Of course some will have access to a magical group and the knowledge and collective experience to be found therein; but for many this will not be the case. Magical groups regardless of hue by and large have much to commend them, but not all of them do. I have in the past been approached by people who have gone through a coven system yet then been led to ask me to help them practice and study magic. It seemed their coven did not in fact practice the arte; which left me wondering what was it that they did do. I am aware of similar approaches made to other magical practitioners, which has left me concluding that some magical groups and covens can actually be detrimental to an individual's magical development and understanding - although this is certainly not the case with all by any means.

Foundations of Practical Sorcery goes some way to rectifying this deficit in any student's magical life. They offer clear magical instruction and accounts of magical acts to be performed, thus making the arte easily accessible. The methods and techniques presented are all based upon my own personal knowledge and experience which goes back over forty years, methods and techniques that have worked successfully for me and will do so for any reader who applies them accordingly.

In many ways I was fortunate, during the autumn of 1972, to meet a magical practitioner who taught me much regarding the arte, generously affording me the run of their magical library as well. Having been schooled extensively in magical knowledge from my mid teen years I consider myself to have been extremely fortunate and lucky to have had many experiences not easily available to many people. Thus the present Foundations of Practical Sorcery series is the distillation of four decades of successful magical workings.

Each of the seven volumes gives a clear account and rendition of one or another area of magical instruction that I have received and have been taught. They are presented to the reader in a clear and workable style which will provide them with a concise and firm foundation, allowing the serious magical student to explore the Western Magical Tradition, the inheritance of us all.

Gary St. M. Nottingham, February 2015

CHAPTER ONE

'Art thou willing to suffer, in order to learn'

This work is the result of some forty years' study, practice and experience of the sorcerous arte. Some of the experiences and the subject matter herein will be considered questionable by some people, but to my mind they are valid. Too much today which is weak, confused and frankly laughable gets passed off for magical practice. Do you, dear reader, think that such fluff-ball practices thought of as being occult today actually are? Where is the *'Witch of Endor'*, when we need her? Instead we have *'Sabrina, the teenage witch'* with which, I feel, I have made my point! The occult arte is what it says it is, occult; that is, secret.

It cannot be bought for money, it must be studied, struggled with. It can be feared, hated or loved, but once your foot is on the road it must be your life, if you are to succeed in any measure. No half-hearted attempts, or weak nonsense and play-acting, will bring success. Determination, persistence and patience are the keys.

People become involved for a variety of reasons: some are noble - *'I desire to know in order to serve'* - for others it is different. Some are simply drawn to it because it is their destiny. There will be those who feel it is the answer to their life's problems and will provide them with an easy life and there are those also who are weak-minded, inadequate and simply inferior and think that the occult will prop them up and give them an identity. But there are also those who simply just want power, and/or knowledge of and the experience of divinity, however you want to perceive it.

But whatever it is that brings you into contact with the occult, what is important is what you are going to do with it. If you ignore it, and it is your destiny, then you can be sure that fate will bring about a situation where you are no longer able to resist. It could be that your life is then turned upside down and events seem to take a turn for the worse. If so, welcome them, because you have been accepted and your fate is acknowledging you. This might seem an odd thing to say, but in my experience and from conversations with others it is only too true. Naturally, there are those who come into the occult with abilities highly developed, but for most people what talents they have will have to be developed and worked upon to gain any measure of success.

We all have abilities to varying degrees in these fields in and they can therefore be developed and above all used. But how? Firstly, we are looking at psychic sensitivity, visualisation skills, concentration abilities and above all, willpower. No will - No power. We all have these abilities, but they must be tested and honed to a cutting edge. The problem is that magical exercises are boring. That's part of the challenge of them; it is part of their power too, because sticking with them develops your determination and your will. Granted there are times when they will be difficult to perform due to pressures of home life or work for example.

But the challenge is to stay with them. You are, are you not, willing to suffer to learn? I remember thirty years ago when I was a keen devotee of the Egyptian Sun God Ra I wanted to organise my day so that I could spend half an hour or so meditating and connecting with the energies of this deity, but the only time that it was quiet in the house with two small boys and the demands of day-to-day living, was five o'clock in the morning. So for months on end I got up at this time, washed, and prepared myself for the work. It meant going to bed earlier at night so that I could do it, which wasn't, in itself, such a bad thing.

There are as we all know, twenty-four hours in the day. If you take eight of them for sleep and eight for work somewhere out of the other eight you ought to be able to find, say, half an hour for magical work and some time for a little magical study. It won't do much at all for your social life, but it will for your inner one. If you want to hang out down at the pub in your spare time or can't wait for the weekend rave then this work is not for you. Whilst I'm not suggesting that you need to live the life of a hermit, once you are on this path then you have other priorities which the general mass of humanity would not understand, so say nothing. One of the things about the sorcerous arte is that it marks you down as being different from most of the rest of your fellow humans, which is no bad thing in some respects. There is now only one way to go, only one way that will suffice and that is forward. There can be no going back.

Despite problems, which must be seen as tests, you must continue with your studies and practices. It is the only way. *There are lions in the way'* as the late magician, W.E. Butler once said. The best place to start is obviously at the beginning, so having made up your mind that the sorcerous and torturous path is for you then, so mote it be.

You will now need to set yourself some time aside, so let's now start to use it. Sitting comfortably somewhere quiet, whether crossed-legged with back straight, or in your favourite yoga asana, let us begin.

Breathe in deep and deeper still, feel the capacity of your lungs. Not only are they filling up with air - you are filling up with the life force and imbibing the prana, as our Eastern brethren would say.

As you breathe out now start to relax, let the tensions of the body cease and be at peace. Breathe in and breathe out to your own body's natural rhythm, don't force it. As the body starts to relax and the tensions cease they will creep back, but release them again and as you do so let the mind relax, let your thoughts now cease. This is, I will be the first to admit, not easy. At first your thoughts will perhaps be silent for a few seconds at best , maybe a little longer. But with practice, you will, in time be able to extend this activity to a minute or even more.

Persistence is the key and let failure be the spur to your success. Practice this simple but important task. Probably for weeks you will not get very far, you are after all developing, what are, shall we say, psychic muscles of which most people are barely aware. It will take time so don't be discouraged. But as time goes by and you persevere, the relaxed states both physically and mentally will deepen.

As they do you will start to notice that your consciousness centres around the area between your eyebrows. If you are in this state and your eyes are open you will observe that you are aware of your surroundings, despite the fact that you are deeply relaxed and not feeling anything, physically, emotionally or mentally. You exist feeling that you are floating. You are neither your feelings nor are you your thoughts, they have been temporary suspended. I know this happens when you go to sleep but in this state when you are awake it is different - you can still perceive your surroundings, you are awake and you are aware.

So if you are in this state and you have demonstrated to yourself that you are therefore not your thoughts nor are you your feelings it then begs the question what are you?

That spark of consciousness that has slipped from out of the silvered sea, that is here right now upon middle earth to experience the trials and tribulations of life in all its entirety; thus allowing it by experience to gain understanding and wisdom with which it can reach attainment to regain its divine birthright as one of the sons or daughters of God. There is much in the *Old Testament* story of the Watchers and the fall of Lucifer from heaven.

When you are closing down from this exercise and are ready to come back to the here and now, wait one moment and visualise yourself, surrounded by the divine brilliance of creation. Feel it, and as you breathe in let it flood into your being with the firm intention that it is a positive health-giving force, which is supercharging you on all levels. Now dwell upon your aura, see it in your mind's eye as being flooded with this energy so much so that you are in an egg of this brilliance. Visualise it with the firm conviction that no negativity can disturb you, nor that your well-being can be disturbed. Feel supercharged and glow. Do not let doubt enter your thoughts. It is this firm conviction that your magic works that will make it so.

Remember those four famous words in the axiom, *'To Know, to Dare, to Will and to keep Silent'*, for such are the words. These are the keys to successful magic. At the end of the day it is not enough to know, it is even simply not enough to dare and neither is it enough to will, for having done and mastered all these arts it is of paramount importance to keep silent. For nothing, but nothing, will succeed like a secret.

Don't talk about what you're about. Stay out of the limelight with your developing skills. Don't let on. When you have performed some magical act and you're letting it gestate, don't tell anyone, just forget about it and let it work. Otherwise you're like a gardener who having planted a seed is constantly digging it up to see what is going on. Once the energies are raised, and have been released, leave them alone from interference and let them go about their work. Constant nagging at them will weaken the flow.

The thing with visualisation is that it is easy to daydream, but it is something else to see something clearly before you and in no uncertain manner so that you treat it as real. You will have to get up to these levels for your magic to work; the goal of your magic must be clearly visualised and powered down the planes to the everyday level. Everything exists first on the subtle levels and must be energised to work on middle earth; otherwise it is just day dreaming and wish-full thinking. You need to work yourself up to fever pitch, to a frenzy, to boil with emotion; then and only then can you supercharge your visualised goal with the power of your intent.

The colour, candles and incense, the consulting of an astrological ephemeris for the most auspicious time, the long, moaning and barbarous words of power are all aids that exalt the senses but in themselves will prove ineffective unless you are completely turned on to your work. You cannot hit it cold. Your magic won't work.

Willpower is also of utmost importance; it is not just wishful thinking. Remember you have a backbone, not a wishbone. The power of your will can be developed. The original followers of the twentieth century magician Aleister Crowleywere infamous because they had a habit, whilst training the will, to cut their arms every time they used the word I. This might seem extreme but seemingly it worked. Discipline yourself to go without something for a given period, something that you want regularly but do not need. I'm sure you can think of something. Give it some thought because, if you break your word to yourself, you may think that it doesn't matter - no one need know or even care come to that - but the deep levels of your being will know:you will be weakening and undermining your willpower, which will not be good for your magic. The everyday will throw up a host of opportunities to strengthen your willpower. Simply getting the best of an argument, particularly where persistence wears the opposition down, has been a traditional training technique of developing the will. Try this first with little things, things that are not of any real consequence. However one word of warning - don't take on anything where commonsense tells you that you don't have a hope in hell of winning; you'll be wasting your time and undermining yourself.

Remember there are two goals to your developing arte: deepening your awareness of divinity and developing your magical skills so that you can bend the bendable. Your ambition is to be a sorcerer/ess not God, there is a difference. In cultivating your magical will you must know what it is that you want, narrow down your field of intention to that one thing, and keep it before your awareness all the time. Then go and get it. *'As my will, So mote it be'*; faith in yourself and the outcome is also of great importance.

Without faith in your workings then your magic is doomed to failure before you start. As adepts have said in the past, *'Faith is the vice in which you hold your crucible will, into which you pour the molten metal of your virulent imagination;'* Faith allows you to know of the inevitability of the success of your magical operations; willpower that will brook no opposition to its goal, a faith that knows that this is so. Paracelsus once said, *'Through faith the imagination is invigorated and completed, for it happens that every doubt will mar its perfection'.*

One of the things about human nature is that we are all suggestible; you may not think that this is so, but it is true. You only have to find a means of getting past the conscious levels and into the deeps of your, or anyone else's mind for your suggestions to gestate and take effect. Look at the power of advertising: if there is no need for a product and people are subsequently not buying it, then the manufacturers call in the advertisers to create a demand. How do they do this? By creating success imagery or promoting the sense that you are a failure if you don't have the latest whatever it is that they are selling. The cynical use of sex or emotion is another tool used, or the appeal to our supposed better natures.

We are all truly suggestible; you just need to pitch it right. So how can we use this to our advantage and to develop our magical abilities?

Having pointed out that we are suggestible we are now going to use it for development. The constant repetition of a simple statement will bring results, maybe not overnight, but with our old friends faith and persistence, they will surely come about. A good time for such practices is when you are just going to sleep or waking up, when you are at the crossroads between worlds. Lying there dozy and drowsy, the barriers are slightly relaxed, the conscious mind is not so alert and things can then slip by and take root.

The trick with this is to keep your sentence short. Come up with something that says all that needs to be said in a plain and unambiguous phrase, something that is positive about what it is that you want. For instance, *'I can visualise clearly, I can visualise strongly;'* not something on the lines of, *'I wish I could visualise better than I can do now'.* Such an approach will get you nowhere with your subconscious mind and is doomed to failure. If you affect things on the inner levels then by and by they will manifest on the outer too. This is a good but simple technique to use to develop your powers of concentration, visualisation, clairvoyant abilities and other psychic sensibilities. Even non-occult potentials such as bad habits, health and the like can be worked on to positive ends. At the end of the day, magic would not be magic if it couldn't help you to improve your magic. There are of course, other methods that can be used that are of a magical nature to help with the development of magical abilities, such as candle magic, which will be discussed later.

The development of a magical persona is a clever way to boost your magic and indeed it is not unknown to use this in the everyday world when confronted with a challenging situation. Go back now to your relaxed state as mentioned earlier. Dwell upon the attributes of, say, firmness and a resolute nature: someone who brooks no interference with their will. Now see yourself as such, feel it, and in your mind's eye experience the sensation of being so. Know that this is you and let it be so. Give this imagery a name or a word, one that is easily remembered, one that you share with no one under any circumstances. Build this imagery up, frequently at first and impress upon yourself that, at the saying of the name, you and the attributes that it represents are one. Do not let the imagery be built up outside yourself - we are not, at this stage, creating servitors or thought forms. Gently and determinedly let the imagery sink down into the depths of your being. Thus the power of your word will flow.

CHAPTER TWO

'Properly prepared, I must be...'

In magic it can be said that timing is invariably everything. You would no more swim against the tides, if you've got any sense, than try to fly to the moon (although I'm told that's been done). There are seasons and times that, when judged aright, can greatly assist the success of your magic. The tides of creation are affected by the movement of the sun, the moon and the stars. Whilst I would not say that the sun and the moon are the actual sources of the power, they are the primary indicators of its ebb and flow throughout creation. Taking them into consideration is a prudent thing to do. As Shakespeare says in *Julius Caesar*, *'There is a tide in the affairs of men, Which taken at the flood leads on to fortune'*.

It is common knowledge in the occult world, but needs to be repeated here, that the time from new to full moon, the waxing moon, is the time to begin and work on creative and positive magical projects. This is a time to build up and promote growth or gain. On the other hand the waning moon, that is from just after the full, down to the new moon, is the time for banishing or the binding of someone or something. This is the time to get rid of as opposed to acquire. But the last quarter and particularly the few days running up to the new moon, the dark of the moon, is for me the most potent time of the moon's cycle. Strangely enough this is the time when I feel at my best, it is also the most vibrant time for cursing someone or contacting the dead.

Having pointed out the importance of timing that the moon has in our practices, it will be somewhat self-defeating to practice outside these times, particularly in the early stages of your studies - although those who have reached a high level of skill in the occult artes will not be hampered by such considerations.

The solar cycle too can be harnessed to our work. The four great solar fire festivals are:

- All Hallows, on 31 October

- Candlemas, on 2 February

- Beltane, on 1 May

- Lammas, on 2 August

These, and the lesser but no less potent times of the summer and winter solstices and the vernal and autumnal equinoxes, are powerful times to launch magical projects.

At these times in the solar cycle, the success of any work done can be greatly enhanced. These festivals mark the stations of the sun's journey: owing to the angle of the earth, as the earth travels around the sun, the sun appears to travel north across the equator, then south, to a point south of the equator. At its most southerly point is the shortest day in the northern parts of the globe. As it travels north it crosses the equator on the 21 March, the Vernal Equinox (equinox literally meaning equal night), when day and night are of equal length.

Before this, the halfway point is reached at Candlemas. After this, the sun travels north and reaches its farthest point on its northern journey on the 21 June, the longest day. Prior to that, the halfway mark from the crossing of the equator to its highest point is on Mayday. At the longest day the sun turns and heads south, again crossing the equator on the 21 September, the Autumnal equinox. The halfway point of the sun travelling from the longest day position to the Autumnal Equinox comes at Lammas. Finally the sun, having crossed the equator south, journeying to its most southerly point, which it will reach on the shortest day, crosses its halfway mark at All Hallows. The sun's journey goes ever on, from the young days of the earth until the earth is no more.

Other times that are relevant to the success of your sorcery are the observing of the sign that the moon is in, particularly for the practice of elemental magic. The moon will travel through every sign of the zodiac in its monthly journey round the earth. Take note. If the moon is in an earthy sign - Capricorn, Taurus or Virgo - then these are good times for the working of earth magic. When the moon is in the watery signs of Pisces, Cancer or Scorpio these are powerful times for working with the water element. Likewise for the fire signs Aries, Leo and Sagittarius, and the air signs Gemini, Libra and Aquarius. Whilst magic involving the elements can be worked outside these times, where possible it is prudent to take note of the better times, when the energies of the cosmos will be flowing in your favour. This is again, I admit, more relevant in the early stages of your career.

The planetary timings are also of importance when working with their energies. The planets can be associated with the days of the week thus:

- Sun-Sunday

- Moon-Monday

- Mars-Tuesday

- Mercury-Wednesday

- Jupiter-Thursday

- Venus-Friday

- Saturn-Saturday

Furthermore the hours of the day and night can be split into planetary hours. This is done for a given date by taking the length of time between sunset and sunrise or vice-versa and dividing it into twelve. This will give the length of that day's planetary hour, which, unless it is at the vernal or autumnal equinox, will not have exactly sixty minutes in it. As there are more hours between sunrise and sunset in the summer than in the winter the daytime planetary hour at this time of the year will have some seventy or more minutes to it and the night-time planetary hour will have less than sixty.

Regardless of the time of year you are working out the length of the planetary hour, the order in which the planets are associated with the twelve planetary hours will be the same. Tradition avers that the following order, and my experience leads me not to question it, is correct. It will also have *'weight'* behind it because it has been used for so long.

The planets associated with the Planetary Hours of the Day from sunrise to sunset starting with the first hour after sunrise each day:

Sunday	Monday	Tuesday	Wednesday	Thursday	Friday	Saturday
Sun	Moon	Mars	Mercury	Jupiter	Venus	Saturn
Venus	Saturn	Sun	Moon	Mars	Mercury	Jupiter
Mercury	Jupiter	Venus	Saturn	Sun	Moon	Mars
Moon	Mars	Mercury	Jupiter	Venus	Saturn	Sun
Saturn	Sun	Moon	Mars	Mercury	Jupiter	Venus
Jupiter	Venus	Saturn	Sun	Moon	Mars	Mercury
Mars	Mercury	Jupiter	Venus	Saturn	Sun	Moon
Sun	Moon	Mars	Mercury	Jupiter	Venus	Saturn
Venus	Saturn	Sun	Moon	Mars	Mercury	Jupiter
Mercury	Jupiter	Venus	Saturn	Sun	Moon	Mars
Moon	Mars	Mercury	Jupiter	Venus	Saturn	Sun
Saturn	Sun	Moon	Mars	Mercury	Jupiter	Venus

The planets associated with the Planetary Hours of the Night from sunset to sunrise starting with the first hour after sunset each night:

Sunday	Monday	Tuesday	Wednesday	Thursday	Friday	Saturday
Jupiter	Venus	Saturn	Sun	Moon	Mars	Mercury
Mars	Mercury	Jupiter	Venus	Saturn	Sun	Moon
Sun	Moon	Mars	Mercury	Jupiter	Venus	Saturn
Venus	Saturn	Sun	Moon	Mars	Mercury	Jupiter
Mercury	Jupiter	Venus	Saturn	Sun	Moon	Mars
Moon	Mars	Mercury	Jupiter	Venus	Saturn	Sun
Saturn	Sun	Moon	Mars	Mercury	Jupiter	Venus
Jupiter	Venus	Saturn	Sun	Moon	Mars	Mercury
Mars	Mercury	Jupiter	Venus	Saturn	Sun	Moon
Sun	Moon	Mars	Mercury	Jupiter	Venus	Saturn
Venus	Saturn	Sun	Moon	Mars	Mercury	Jupiter
Mercury	Jupiter	Venus	Saturn	Sun	Moon	Mars

Planetary days and hours really come into their own when working on talismans or with planetary spirits; and are particularly important when working with evocation, that is calling forth planetary spirits, be it into the speculum (the magical mirror) or manifestation into a triangle.

Lastly, all the planetary hours will have an angel associated with them; these will be the most auspicious times to work with these beings, not that they cannot be contacted at other times.

One occult arte that is kept under wraps is the arte of thought transference. Which, considering its potential for good or ill, will probably be no great surprise. It is a useful technique not only in your magical work, but also in the world of the everyday. Go back now to your relaxed state that we worked with earlier on. Imagine that you are looking at the world from the palm of your hand or another part of your body; imagine that your consciousness is in that part and you are observing the world from that position. After several sessions with this work, try projecting your view of the world from an apple or some other object. When you have got some experience of this, place your consciousness into a dog or cat; look at the world from their viewpoint and see the world through their eyes.

Now try with people: endeavour to place your consciousness into a person, to look at the world through their eyes. Whilst I am not suggesting that you should then will them, from this vantage point, to do something that would be better for them that they didn't, the potential arises to assist or hinder someone. Whatever you do, I would suggest that you would be wise to be very mindful of that fact. This is a good trick to bring someone to you, and one that I can vouch for personally. This trick of projecting consciousness is needed for the exploration of other levels of being. We will also be using it by and by in the consecration and charging of magical tools.

So far you have been working with magic that really can be performed while sitting on your bed. Now we need to move on a bit and start considering some ritual practices.

There will be those who are much taken with ritual practice and drama and I must admit a well-worked piece of sacred drama is something worth seeing. Ritual heightens the senses, amplifies the energy, and promotes success. I remember a Luciferian of my acquaintance once telling me that, when they were training with a well-known name back in the early sixties, one day they were taken to Westminster Roman Catholic Cathedral to watch the mass being performed in its entirety. It was for them a lesson in the drama of ritual. The act of ritual will reinforce the suggestions and the intent of your magic. It becomes the lens that focuses and concentrates the will. Ritual with its sounds and symbols becomes the language of those subconscious levels that are beneath the everyday.

Therefore, with your rituals put some punch into them: don't dither, don't feel embarrassed or foolish, and don't be timid. I'm not saying that you need to bellow so that you can be heard in the next street nor do you need to over-act but things will need to be done with assertion. Let the words roll, feel the intoxication of their power, and let your senses be exalted.

Probably the most well-known ritual in magic is the Lesser Banishing Ritual of the Pentagram, which pops up everywhere; no doubt because it works and works well. Like all good cooks you will need to clear your workplace and this ritual is good for removing the flotsam and jetsam of the psychic levels. With daily practice you will soon get into the flow of it. This work will help to sharpen up your visualisation skills considerably, and be of great use later on in your magical operations. It can also be developed into other acts of invocation and banishment. Learn it and learn it well as it holds the keys to many aspects of ritual magic.

The Lesser Banishing Ritual of the Pentagram

Facing east visualise above your head a glowing ball of divine brilliance, feel it hum and buzz. Even feel that your consciousness is placed there, even if only done momentarily. Let this be your link with the divine and the placing of the following work under the auspices of the highest. Raising your right hand draw down this light through the crown of your head. As this light touches your skull intone the word 'ATEH', meaning 'to thee'. Bring your hand down to your navel, and as you do let the shaft of light descend through you to your feet. When it does, intone 'MALKUTH' ('the kingdom').

Now touch your right shoulder and the word is 'VE-GEBURAH' ('and the power'). Bring your hand across your body and touch the left shoulder and as you do bring the light across from the right to the left shoulder and let the word be 'VE-GEDULAH' ('and the glory'). Visualise the cross that you have formed running through your being and cross hands on your breast intoning 'LE OHLAM AMEN' (for ever Amen).

This first piece of the ritual is known as the Kabbalistic Cross. Normally it is done in Hebrew, but sometimes in Latin.

To continue, still facing east, point your right arm out from your body and with the first two fingers of your right hand trace a large five-pointed star in front of your body with the point facing upwards. Let this star glow with brilliance and as it does stab the centre with your right hand and intone the word 'YHVH' (yod heh vav heh). Trace it from the bottom left corner to the top, then down to the bottom right from where it is traced to the upper left opposite your left shoulder then across to the upper right opposite your right shoulder, from there bring it down to the bottom left where you started. With your mind's eye let this star be pushed to the outer limits of your work area.

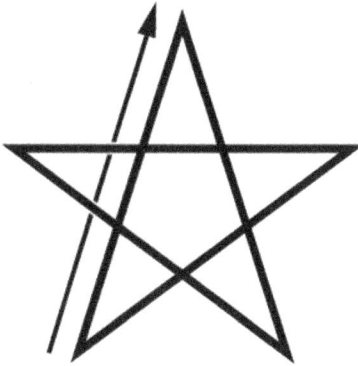

The Banishing Pentagram

Now, still with your arm out-stretched, trace a line in the atmosphere from the right arm of this star to the south. Facing south, you must draw before you another star the same as the last one. This time, as you stab the centre of it, intone the word 'ADNI' (Adoni). Visualise this star moving away from you to connect, at the edge of your workspace, with the line you have traced from the first star.

As before, draw a line in the atmosphere before you and bring it around to the west. Like the last time, trace before you another star. This time the word to be intoned as you stab the centre is 'EHIEH' (eh-heh-yeh). With your mind's eye let the star move to the edge of your workspace and connect with the line that you brought around from the south. From this western pentagram now trace a line to the northern quarter.

As before, trace a pentagram in the air before you. When it is bright and strong in front of you intone the word 'AGLA.' As with the other stars around you, let this one be moved out to the edge of your workspace, where it connects with the line that was brought around from the west. When the northern pentagram is in position bring a line from its arm around to the pentagram in the east, thus completing the circle around you with a glowing pentagram at each quarter.

Now, standing in the centre of your circle, face east and stretch out on either side of you both your arms so that you form a cross. Standing in this position visualise, outside your circle, a vast being dressed in robes of yellow shot through with purples. Feel breezes blowing from this quarter and intone *'Before me Raphael.'* Still standing in this position visualise behind you and outside your circle a large being dressed in blue with orange flashing through the robes. Feel the cool flow of running water from this quarter, and let the words be, *'Behind me Gabriel',* followed by, *On my right Mikael.'* To your right see a large and powerful being dressed in robes of red with green flashes through them. Feel the sensation of heat. Still facing east intone *'On my left, Auriel',* and see in this station a potent figure dressed in the colours of the earth; be aware of the fertility of the earth as you do so.

Now, holding all this imagery, say *'About me flame the pentagrams, behind me shines the six-rayed star.'* At this point feel a glowing six-pointed star on your back. This is made up of two interlocking triangles, one red with its point up, the other blue with its point down, symbolising the conjoining of the opposites; the descent of the higher into the lower, that is man's higher self conjoining and invigorating his lower self, setting a seal on the work. Finally stand facing east and perform the opening Kabbalistic Cross.

Congratulations, you have just performed your first piece of ritual! This rite is used at the opening and closing of many forms of magical ritual. It may seem daunting at first but with daily practice you'll soon get the measure of it. Indeed you could, having performed it, then move on to doing some of the simpler exercises already covered, and gain all round. Having come thus far, we need to move on.

Now that you have some accomplishment with the above ritual, we can start using it for an exploration and connection of the four elements, plus spirit. The four elements air, fire, water and earth, are an integral part of the occult universe. Whilst we may think of them in their physical forms, we need to connect with them on a much more subtle level as they also represent potent energies, energies that have a profound influence on our lives and on our magic. With the next work we will make use of all the benefits of your previous magical exercises.

Firstly you need to acquire a tarot pack; preferably the Rider-Waite pack as these are painted and designed in colours and in such a way that they are extremely potent for this work. One of the more important things about the tarot, which often gets overlooked by the general public, is how they can be used for the exploration of other levels.

The trick, if I can call it that, is to use the cards as doorways to other levels. This has been a well-guarded secret until recent times, but was also discovered quite separately by the Swiss psychologist, Carl Jung.

One day he was travelling up an escalator and, in a semi day-dream state he suddenly saw a poster of an alpine scene on the wall. Wondering what was on the other side of the mountain in the picture, he imagined that he was in the picture and walking up the mountain to see. Jung went on to call this trick *active imagination* and used it a lot with his patients. In fact, what he had done was to use an old occult technique that had been kept well secret. What we are going to do now is very similar.

Making sure that you have somewhere to work undisturbed for a while, take out the ace of air. Note that there are four aces in the pack, one for each element. Facing east perform, as already described, the Kabbalistic Cross and the banishing pentagram ritual.

Place the ace of air in front of you. Now, sitting comfortably, start to relax and empty your mind, getting into a deep relaxed and comfortable state. Imagine that you are surrounded by a brilliant and clear yellow. This is a colour associated with the element air. The other elements are associated with the following colours: red-fire, blue-water and green-earth.

Now, as you breathe in, imagine that you are breathing the air element in, in the form of this yellow colour. Try to feel it, feel the light air properties of this element. When you feel *'loaded'* with this element, look at the ace of air placed conveniently in front of you. Look at it for a couple of minutes. Now close your eyes and see the card in front of you and imagine it to be the size of a door. You must now trace in your mind's eye an invoking pentagram of air over it as the opening gesture and intone the word 'SHADDIA EL CHAI' (shaddey el chay) to define the next part of the work.

You are opening the door so that you can enter. Having done so, feel that you are walking into the card and are actually in the scene. It is customary not to speak to anyone until you are spoken too. Explore the element at this level. Sometimes you can be given answers to problems or gain insight into the working of the element in question. All this work, will, after having been done on several occasions, be of great use in the consecration of yourself and your magical tool kit. Have no fear that you will get lost at this level but do be sure to come back the same way that you went in. Come back through the door and close it. Close it also by tracing the relevant banishing elemental pentagram over the door with the intent that the door is closed. Breathe out the yellow light that you breathed in at the beginning of this work. Stand up and stamp your foot a couple of times to re-establish yourself in the everyday world. Close with the Kabbalistic Cross and the banishing pentagram. It is usual to write up your experiences of each working that you perform which can be useful for future reference.

There is no need to work with all the elements in one week. Explore the same doorway a couple of times and then move on to the next element the following week. By and by you will gain proficiency in this work and the sense of ritual will flow and with that will come the benefits thereof.

Having worked your way through the four elements crown your work with the element spirit. For that there will be no card as a doorway. Instead visualise yourself in an indigo egg, then visualise an indigo egg as the doorway and walk into that. Use both the active and passive pentagrams in opening and closing.

With the other elements use the following words of power:

Fire: YHVH TZABAOTH
(yod heh vav heh tza bay oth) and the colour red.

Water: ELOHIM TZABAOTH
(elohim tza bay oth), colour blue.

Earth: ADNI HA ARETZ
(adonia ha aretz), colour green.

Spirit (active): EXARP EHEIEH
(ex ar peh eh eh, yeh eh heh yeh).

Spirit (passive): HCOMA AGLA
(hec coma, ah gla), colour indigo.

PENTAGRAMS:

The thing with the pentagram symbol is that in the modern occult world it's everywhere - you can't open a book or one of those dreadful occult magazines that seem to be everywhere without tripping over the thing (*The Cauldron* and *Verdelet* excepted). So what's it all about? Often you will see wiccans, witches and Uncle Tom Cobley and all displaying one of these symbols, frequently with very little knowledge regarding its meaning. Before we go on, looking at some of the considerations of this symbol may be a prudent thing to do. The pentagram has five arms, one for each element, with the top arm being equated with spirit, which is considered to rule over the elements. To each of these elements tradition has given a Hebrew letter: yod-fire, heh-water, vav-air and finally heh-earth.

The letter representing spirit is the letter shin. The Western Occult Tradition asserts that these five letters can be arranged to spell the Hebrew name YhshVH = Yeshuvuh, which is I believe the original name of Jesus. In Hebrew there is no J so therefore the name Jesus could not have have been his real name. With the consideration that spirit is the top element on the symbol and dominates the other four, we are now moving into the area of Luciferianism where the Luciferian energies are expelled from on high and are made manifest in the world of matter and rule therein by virtue of its divinity. Therefore the story of Lucifer being expelled from heaven becomes an evolutionary tale of spirit manifesting in matter to speed up its evolution.

This can be symbolized by the reversed pentagram, the descent of spirit into matter; which is a far cry from the idea that the reversed pentagram is a sign of evil. This was promulgated by the 19th century French magus, Eliphas Levi, with his story of the reversed symbol being the devil attacking heaven with his horns. Is this a clever deception with the real meaning hidden for years without anyone cottoning on to it? And if spirit is, shall we say, in exile here on middle earth, here to experience the opposite energies of good and bad, then it is this experiencing and assimilating the lessons learnt that are evolutionary and which allow the individual slowly ever so slowly to set the course of their being for the heavenly realms. Therefore this IS the assault on Heaven; the spirit imprisoned in this body of clay and striving for reunion with its source.

Looking at the general state of human nature it's probably hard to believe that humans are of divine origin, as they seem so asleep to their spiritual side and so ignorant of their divinity. But then you don't have to be the same as the rest of the mindless herd; that's why you are reading this book. In the Kabbalah the first virtue to acquire is that of discrimination, which is inspired by the vision of Malkuth. The vision is an awakening to the fact that you have a divine side to your nature, and this needs to be acknowledged and expressed. The vice associated with this is inertia, that is being in ignorance of your spirituality and doing nothing about it. Although being in ignorance of it doesn't put you in a position to do anything about it, you will remain there until you are made aware of the possibility of something far greater than yourself, something compared to which you are a speck.

Having thus come this far we are now getting ready for the

acquisition of various occult implements, which will be put to good use with ritual in due course. There are several things that you will have to acquire.

Firstly, a knife with a black hilt. You can paint the hilt black if it is not. This can be associated with the element air.

Secondly, a wooden stick for a wand; this is the magical weapon of the fire element. For this I recommend that you hunt down a suitable tree, hazel is good as it has fire element associations. Find a branch about 1" thick and the length of the distance between your elbow and the tip of your middle finger. When you have found the right branch then spend some time with the tree and explain what you are about, then on a waxing moon make the effort to get out of bed early and cut the branch at sunrise. Leave a token payment of something in acknowledgment of the tree spirit. Now you must peel the branch. Some folks will either drill a hole right down the middle and insert a magnetized rod or animating fluid (discussed later), or cut along the length of the rod thus leaving a groove the whole length of it and then inserting the necessary and then filling it over with wood filler or such like. It can be painted black and bound around the middle with red cotton, or some such. Having said that, I've also known wands that have simply had a piece of obsidian stone inserted in their tip which will work just as well. I'm sure there are also those who have done none of these things and still get good results.

But whatever you choose to do, it will be more personal and pokey if you anoint it with some of your blood. This will help to deepen the bond and make it special, as will this practice with all your magical regalia.

A chalice is the obvious symbol of the element water and as such silver would be a good choice although pottery or wood will work well.

For a pentacle, the outward expression of the earth element, a 6" disc of copper or brass is ideal. Clay is the obvious choice as is wood or beeswax. Whatever material you use it will have to be engraved or painted accordingly.

Also needed will be a black robe with hood, easy enough to make, just have a little patience, and it will be the better for you having made it yourself. Take a black piece of cloth say three feet wide and ten feet long or thereabouts and fold it in half long ways so that you have reduced it to five feet in length, you will now have the back and the front of your robe. Cut a hole for your head to go through and sew up the sides leaving space for your arms. Two sleeves can be made as two cloth tubes the length of your arms and sewn in place. The hood is quite easy too. Depending on how big your head is, fold, say, a three-foot square into a triangle. This, sewn up on one side, which will be the back, and sewn appropriately into the neck of your robe should do it. It doesn't have to win first prize in your local W. I. tent but make some effort and do it with a little bit of pride. Now wash it and if possible leave it outside to dry. When washing it do it with the intent that all past influences are being washed away, wash it by hand and add a little salt to the water. With this robe on, you shed your everyday personality to become something else.

An altar is simple enough. This is your magical worktop, the table before the High Ones. This needs to be about waist high, it could be made from plywood and painted black; alternatively find something suitable. When you do, wash it down with salt water and if you have some hyssop growing in your garden add a little of that too. Wash it with the intent that all past influences are being removed and it is being dedicated to the success of your magics.

Candle sticks are another essential. Definitely two for your altar and four if it is felt needed to mark the compass points. As with your robe and altar, clean these with intent: after all, if you are buying them second-hand you do not know what they have picked up in their lives and if you are buying from one of the many New Age shops that are around it will still be prudent to do the same, particularly from what I've seen of some of them.

Candles, charcoal and incense; when it comes to buying these consumables, I don't think that you can beat the church supply shops. After all, the church has been around for quite some time and it only uses the best, although frankly it seems to me to be wasted on the congregations and the half-tutored priesthood, but that's their business. None of that dreadful Nag Champa joss stick or any other hippy stuff.

A censer will of course also be required. Hunt about. Some authorities suggest a clay flowerpot with sand in or even a lump of plasticene with a joss stick in it. I don't think so. Do not spoil the ship for a ha'porth of tar. You will find in the church supply shops a variety of swing chain censers; also your local new age shop is probably going to have one, so a suitable censer should not be too hard to acquire.

A second wand is also needed. This represents your will and is therefore a symbol thereof. Cut, on a waxing moon, a straight ash branch or one from an almond tree, if you can find one. Observe the usual protocols as with your fire wand. Peel it and let it dry. Link it with your life force via your blood and dress the wand with the oil of Abra-Melin, (this oil will be discussed shortly).

The sword. In the past I have made these in the manner of the ones depicted in the *Key of Solomon* from a three-foot flat piece of mild steel. If you want to do likewise you will have to find yourself a steel supplier. Alternatively buy one (a sword not a steel supplier). The sword is a tool of power and is used where a strong level of assertion is needed such as in the evoking of a spirit. There are also other workings where it is appropriate, cursing for example, to name but one. I'm alsomindful that the Wiccans wave them around at initiations for some reason, but that is not relevant to us. Having gained your sword; clean it as we have said elsewhere and anoint it with your life blood to establish the link that will make it yours.

You will also need a dip pen as your pen of arte and a variety of coloured inks, an appropriate one for each for each of the planetary energies. Parchment for talismans is also useful. Other things like herbs and tinctures will be dealt with accordingly.

The Script of Honorius

This is an old magical script sometimes called Theban, and can be found in Agrippa. Wherever it originated, it is a script that we will use a lot, so you will do well to learn it, which isn't a hard thing to do. Try writing out each letter twenty or thirty times on a regular basis and write your shopping list out with it - you'll soon learn. I should leave Runes to the Rune Master, Ogham to the Celt and Hebrew to the Kabbalistic scholar, for us the script of Honorius will serve our sorcerous arte well.

Having come this far your kit will need consecrating and dedicating to the success of your arte. Whilst there are several ways of doing this, it is going to be useful to know why and a method of how. The reason for doing this is simple; you are marking it out from the everyday things of your life, you are making it special. Also you are clearing out any occult flotsam and jetsam that the object has picked up in its former life, before you came along. You are also wanting to bond with it, to make it a part of you. This is where all your past endeavours will start to pay off. So far you have been getting ready for this and what comes after.

Having been working through the elemental work given earlier you are now in a better position to charge your magical kit. There is one thing that we haven't covered so far, the working space. The ideal space of a room set to one side and kept locked from prying eyes is ideal, more so if you have space in it for a nine-foot circle and a three-foot triangle for evocation as suggested in the *Key of Solomon*. But many of us do not have that living space spare, so we have to make do. Mercifully, Solomon points out that you can equally use old ruined castles, buildings or a secluded wood. This is fine, if it's handy. The thing is that you do not want to be disturbed.

In Israel Regardie's masterpiece *The Tree of Life* there is the tale of someone who uses the beach at Eastbourne of all places to evoke an undine from the sea, although, with so many people retiring there, necromancy shouldn't be too hard. Anyway, if I remember aright what happened was that in the middle of the night the sorcerer was at his work on the beach in the fogs and mists as they rolled in off the sea, the only thing that he summoned with his long barbarous names of power and clouds of incense was a policeman who wanted to know what he was doing. A salutary lesson no doubt! So find somewhere where you are not going to be interrupted.

Other than that you will have to use your living space, so move the furniture out of the way. Clear a space and sweep it clean, with intent. I suggest that you take off your shoes to do this and keep the workspace as something different from the everyday whilst in use.

The circle can be marked out in chalk, flour, or white tape. Sometimes it is painted on a large bed sheet and pegged down or, if you have somewhere permanent, painting it on the floor will do fine. For our work a nine-foot diameter circle is what is needed, with an inner one at eight and a half feet although if this space is not available then make it whatever size you can move around in comfortably. The six inches between the two circles will give you ample room to mark out in between the lines the relevant names of power, which govern the work that you are performing. Names have a power of their own and need to be respected as such. The circle, which is neither in this world or the next, will be your living symbol of divinity and as such will reflect creation, that is, it is creation in miniature, with you at the centre.

If you are using any everyday objects clean them before magical use. With a little intent and a declaration that it is holy, a little salt water with hyssop in will be found useful when wiping things clean of all past associations.

Cover your altar with a cloth specially kept and dedicated for such work. This can be in the elemental or planetary colour relevant to the work. A black cloth overlaid with a white one will prove effective for work of a positive nature; reverse the colour scheme if working negatively.

CHAPTER THREE

'Armed at all points'

Now that you have got together all your magical tools and requirements; and having also been working at magical exercises and elemental workings, we can move on to the consecrating and dedicating of your tools of arte. Firstly do not be englamoured by the trappings of magic. The flickering candle light with the billowing clouds of incense, the long wordy invocations and not forgetting, your ego.

Magic is a heady subject and it is easy to lose your sense of the mundane and the everyday world. For you it must be more important than for most people to balance your life in the everyday with your magical activities. Sorcerers/esses with their heads in the clouds and their feet not firmly on the ground are of no use to themselves or anyone else. Having said that let's push on. Take a bath with a little salt therein and hyssop if available. Lie in the bath and intone solemnly:

> *'Asperges me Domine hyssopo, et mundabor, lavabis me, et super nivem dealbabor'*
>
> *(Purge me with hyssop O Lord, and I shall be clean, wash me and I shall be whiter than snow).*

Wash yourself with the knowing that the woes and the worries of life are being left behind. Now robe with the intent that you are putting on your other self. This can be marked with the old wording:

> *'By the figurative mystery of these holy vestments, I will clothe me with the armour of salvation in the strength of the most high! Ancor; Amacor; Amides; Theodonias; Anitor; that my desired end may be effected through thy strength, O Domini! Unto whom the praise and the glory will belong forever. So mote it be.'*

Take your altar, its cloth, candlesticks and your censer and on a waxing moon set them up in your workspace facing east. Declare that this is their dedication to the success of all your magical endeavours. Perform the banishing ritual that you used earlier with your elemental workings.

Raising your right hand over the censer say:

'Blessings be upon thee O censer, let all malignancy be cast forth hence from, so only the power of on high may enter herein, unto the success of my magics. Hear my words addressed to thee, for this my will, so mote it be'.

Let a stream of brilliance pour forth from your hand and be absorbed by the censer, see it glow with divine brilliance. Anoint the censer with the oil of Abra-Melin. Now use the censer.

Changing the relevant pieces of equipment and the wording accordingly use this rite for your altar, its cloths, candlesticks and candles. Close this simple rite with the following:

'Non nobis Domini non nobis, sed nomini tuo da honorum, Propter benignitatem tuam, propter fide tuam'

(Not unto us O Lord not unto us, but unto thy name be the glory for your mercy and faith).

Finish with the banishing ritual that you used in the beginning and declare:

'Domine unam est'… (The Lord is one).

Whilst I am the first to admit that I can only command a rudimentary school-boy Latin, I am aware of the magical potential of the language, as it has been used as a ritual language in the west, like Sanskrit has in the east for many years. Latin has, over the centuries, built up quite a reservoir of power, which mercifully the New Agers and the Wiccan Wannabees have overlooked. However I note certain satanic groups and individuals seem to be aware of it. Although I am not suggesting that all your rituals should be in Latin, its judicious use at sensitive points will add a little extra to your workings.

It is wise to keep all pieces of ritual equipment wrapped up and out of the sight of the profane. From now on they do not belong to this world for they are of another order. Be mindful of this and treat them as such.

Use also a wording and a dedication on your candles before use, as they will need to be consecrated to the success of your arte. Candles can be used more than once, particularly on the repetition of a piece of work, but it is not advisable to use the same candles that have been used say for a Saturnine operation for another type of work as the two energies will not work successfully together.

Taking your magical knife, on a waxing moon bury it somewhere and remember where it is! Dig it up after three days and nights, and clean it. If you have an astrological ephemeris and can work out when the moon is in an air sign so much the better for our work, but if not we can manage without, providing we are still on a waxing moon of course. Find a quiet time and clear your working space as already suggested.

Set up an altar and place thereon the black hilted knife, a censer, (burn some good quality church incense or if unavailable use frankincense), a pair of white candles, with candlesticks plus some salt and a clean glass of water. Cover your altar with a clean white cloth and let the altar face towards the east.

Facing towards the east declare your intent.

Light your charcoal and be mindful because it can spit and burn.

Contemplate the work in hand for a few moments.

Declare:

> 'Be thou far from me O thou profane!'
> 'I proclaim a working invoking the element air that this athana (the magical knife) may be made holy unto the success of all my magics'.

Having lit your candles and incense, perform the banishing ritual.

Now facing east, pour the salt into your left hand and point the first two fingers of your right hand at it, see a brilliant stream of light pour into the salt from your two fingers, and say the words of hallowing:

> 'Ego, benidictus salsus in nomine Deo et per divinitatis mea'
> (I bless this salt in the name of God and by my divinity).

Salt only needs to be blessed, because of its holy and preservative power it is considered already to be consecrated. Pointing again with the same two fingers at the water in the clean glass, see the brilliance pour into it as with the salt whilst saying:

> 'Te exorcizo per Dei omnipotentis virtutem qui regnat per saecula saeculorum'
>
> (I exorcise you by the almighty living god who is king by the holy of holies).

Now pour the salt into the water and advance to the eastern boundary of your working space. Travelling sunwise, deosil, sprinkle the waters at the edge as you walk around it, intoning:

> 'Let the sorcerer/ess, sprinkle with the lustral waters of the loud resounding sea'

Now carry your censer likewise.

> 'After all the phantoms have vanished, thou shalt see that holy and formless fire, that fire that flashes through the hidden depths of the universe, hear thou the voice of fire'.

Having made your clockwise circumambulations come back to the centre of the circle.

Perform the opening cross as in the beginning of the banishing ritual.

Go to the eastern edge of your circle and there, facing outward, trace with the first two fingers of your right hand the invoking pentagram of air thus:

Air

Visualise this figure in bright yellow, and as you trace it intone firmly:

> 'Oro-bah-heh-ao-zod-pi'.

This is the Enochian name that governs the element air and the eastern quarters. It is pronounced as *'Ero-ebah-hay-ao-zod-pay'*.

Stab the centre of the figure and intone the word YHVH. Gaze into the figure before you and see through it and into the realms of the air. See the winds and the clouds blowing about, feel the breeze and in your best magical voice say:

> 'Ye mighty ones of air, for I do summon thee from where thou art to witness this rite and to guard this sacred space of mine, from all perils that do approach from the east.'

With your hand still raised trace a line in brilliance from the pentagram around to the southern quarter. Here repeat the working, using the appropriate invoking elemental pentagrams. Trace your circle around to the west and the north, repeating the working for each direction, returning back to where you started in the east. Return to the centre and visualise a complete circle about you. Now standing in the centre of your space, visualise, as you did in the banishing ritual, the figures at the compass points and intone their names. Feel their presence, know that they are there.

As with this work and all other magical working, an expression of your own divinity and an acknowledgement of the higher is always germane to the work at this point.

Therefore say with conviction:

> 'Blessed art thou Lord of creation
> for thy glory flows out unto the ends of being for all time.
> Be with me now whilst I perform this work
> which I dedicate unto thee.'

To acknowledge your *'connection with divinity'* intone the following. It's not gobbley-gook but a time-honoured Enochian invocation which is not to be treated without respect.

I give also a translation of the work, as it is no bad thing to know what it is that you are saying:

> 'OL SONUF VAORSAGI GOHO IADA BALTA
> ELEXARPEH COMANANU TABITOM
> ZODAKARA EKA ZODAKARE OD ZODA MERANU
> ODO KIKLE QAA PIAPE PIAMOEL OD VAOAN'.

Pronounced as follows:

> 'Oh-ell soh-noof vay-oh-air-sah-jee goh-hoh ee-ahdah bal-tah.
> EL-EX-AR-PAY-HAY CO-MAH-NAH-NOO TAH-BEE-TOH-EM.
> Zohd-ah-kah-rah eh-kah. Zoh-ah-kah-ray oh-dah.
> Zohd-ah-mer-ah-noo.
> Oh-doh kee-klay kah-ah pee-ah-pay pee-ah-moh-ell oh-dah vay-oh-ahnoo'

Meaning:

> 'I reign over you saith the God of justice.
> ELEXARPEH COMANANU TABITOM.
> (these are the three angels who rule over the Tablet of Union
> from the Enochian system).
> Move therefore and show yourselves.
> Appear unto us; open the mysteries of thy creation,
> the balance of righteousness and truth'.

Still in the middle of your working space and facing the eastern quarter, intone this general invocation to the higher powers for the hallowing of your working space:

> 'I invoke thee, O ye angels of the celestial spheres
> whose dwelling is in the invisible.
> For thou art the guardians of the gates of the universe
> be thou the guardians of this my sacred space.
> Keep far removed from me the evil and the unbalanced.
> Strengthen and inspire me so that I may preserve unsullied
> this abode of divinity.
> Let my sphere be pure that I may enter therein and become
> a partaker of the secrets of the light divine.'

Contemplate the sanctity and the sacredness of your space for a few moments. Make sure that the thurible hasn't run out of incense, at this point.

Trace over the athana, in the air an invoking air pentagram and declare what you are about. Say:

> 'In and by the holy name
> Shaddai-el-Chai, (pronounced as Shaddie-el-Chay),
> and by the might of the holy archangel Raphael.
> And in the name of the mighty angel of the holy element air,
> Chassan
> and also by the power of the king of the spirits of air
> Paralda
> do I invoke the energies of the element air
> to assist in this the consecration of the holy athana
> to the success of my magical arte'.

Sprinkle the knife with some of your consecrated water and, declaring that all past associations are now washed away and that the knife is made fit for its hallowing, hold it in the rising incense smoke saying:

> 'I do bless, consecrate and dedicate this knife
> to be the holy athana of mine arte
> and it will aid the success of all my magics.
> So Mote It Be'.

If you are going to anoint the knife with your life force then do it now. Draw blood with a clean and sterile point or blade. As you now breathe in feel your body, starting with the feet and working upwards, filling up with the element air depicted as a yellow mist that feels light and airy. When you have filled up your being with this energy invoke the holy names of the air element in the order given above declaring again your intent. Pick up the knife, and pour into it via your right hand, if right-handed (use left if left-handed) all the accumulated energies of the element air.

See them hover around and about the knife. Let the knife absorb them and glow with its power. At this point endeavour to place your consciousness into the knife; try to look out at the world from the knife and be the knife. Return to normal awareness. Pick up the athana and trace an invoking pentagram in the air with it, whilst declaring that this athana is now made holy and is dedicated to the success of your magic.

Give the words of banishment and thanks:

> *'I do give thanks to the holy element air*
> *and to the mighty name YHVH,*
> *and also to the archangel Raphael,*
> *and I do give thanks to the angel of air Chassan*
> *and to the king Paralda*
> *for assisting me in this my holy act of magic.*
> *Let there be grace, harmony and peace*
> *between thee and me now and for always,*
> *for I too am a servant of the God most high'*

Facing east still, declare the following:

> *'Non nobis Domini non nobis,*
> *Sed nomini tua da honorum.*
> *Propter benignatatum. Propter fidi tuam'.*

Perform the air banishing ritual of the pentagram. To do so, do as you did in the beginning at the invoking, repeating it with the same name and colours but reversing the flow of the pentagram thus:

Declare:

> *'Domine Unam Est, The Lord is One'*

Use this given format and change the elemental names, colours and the flow of the pentagrams accordingly.

Element	Colour	God Name	Archangel	Angel	King
Air	Yellow	Shaddia El Chai	Raphael	Chassan	Paralda
Fire	Red	YHVH Tzabaoth	Mikael	Aral	Djinn
Water	Blue	Elohim Tzabaoth	Gabriel	Taliahad	Niksa
Earth	Green	Adoni ha-Aretz	Uriel	Phorla	Ghob

Always clean your magical equipment first before the consecration takes place.

The following runes have always been traditional in some quarters for inscribing on your magical knife and are from the *Greater Key of Solomon*:

Athana runes:

Chalice:

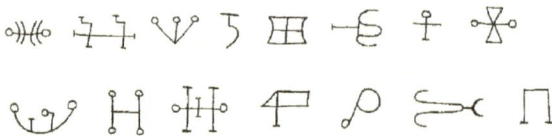

Wand:

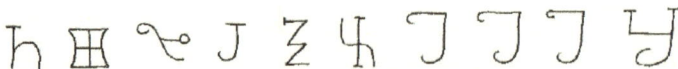

Pantacle:

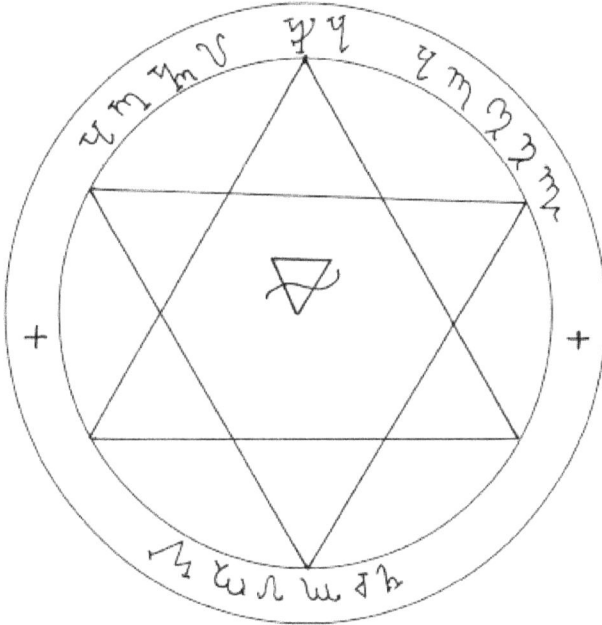

This is a design for the front with the God Names for earth at the top, with the archangel and angel names around the side. They are written in the Theban script. On the other side will be your magical name expressed as a sigil. To create this, write down the name and then cross out any letters that repeat themselves. Then combine the remainder into a shape that represents the secret name. Let this be the sigil of thy secret being.

Using these methods of consecration you can quietly work through the charging of your magical kit. As for the sword and the wand (not the fire wand) we will be dealing with these by and by as they are extremely important tools when working with evocations and spirits. Other wands are useful with herb work and the concocting of potions and will be dealt with in a similar manner.

So far you have constructed and hallowed circles of power for each element, which is fine if working with a particular element but for other magical work we will have to approach things a little differently.

All ritual work that you perform will need to be started off with the Lesser Banishing Ritual of the Pentagram as given earlier and the consecration of the working space with water and fire as shown, although these methods will vary with different practitioners.

What follows is a basic ritual format that I have found to work and work well. It is an adaptation of various techniques from a variety of sources. Firstly, as in the beginning, clear your working area and perform the Lesser Banishing Ritual of the Pentagram. Then proceed to consecrate the space with fire and water as you have been shown. The compass points will be hallowed as in the following manner. Perform the opening gesture of the cross as in the Lesser Banishing Ritual of the Pentagram, then go to the eastern quarter and trace before you with your athana the invoking pentagram of air. As you do so see it form in yellow and intone the words:

'Oro ebah aozodpi'

Pronounced as:

'Oro-eheh-bah-heh-ao-zodpeh.'

Stab the centre and as you do so intone:

'Yod-heh-vav-heh.'

Look into the pentagram and see the element air being active. Saying:

'Oh thou holy and wise eagle,
great ruler of storms and whirlwind,
Master of the heavens and prince of the power of air.
Be present, O ye mighty ones of the East
and assist me in this my holy act of magic.'

Feel the winds blow. Now trace around to the south a bright and blazing circle and here trace a red invoking pentagram of fire, intoning:

'Oip teaa pedoce.'

Pronounced as:

'Oh-ee-pay tay-ah-ah pay-doh-kay.'

Stab the centre saying *'Elohim'*. Look into the heart of the pentagram and see fire being active. Feel the heat and see the flames. Saying:

'O thou lion, Lord of Lightnings,
Great prince of the powers of fire
be present we pray thee
and assist in this my act of holy magic.'

Now carrying on to the western point trace a line in brilliance. Here draw in the air an invoking water pentagram tracing it in blue. As you are drawing it intone:

'Em Peh Arsel Gaiol.'

Pronounced as:

'em-pay-hay ar-sel gah-ee-ohl. '

Stab the centre saying:

'El'

Look into the pentagram and see the power of water, see the crash and the roar of the sea. And say:

'O thou serpent of old, ruler of the deeps,
Guardian of the bitter sea
Prince of the powers of water
be present O ye mighty ones of the west
and assist with this my act of magic.'

Now bring the line around to the north, here trace another pentagram before you in the air. This will be the invoking earth one and is drawn in green intoning:

'Emor dial hectega'

Pronounced:

'Ee-mor dee-ahl hec-tay-gah.'

Stab the centre declaring *'Adoni'*. Look into the pentagram and see the earth in all its glory, the richness and the fertility thereof, saying:

'Black bull of the north, horned one,
dark ruler of the mountains and all that lies beneath them.
Prince of the powers of earth,
be present O ye mighty ones of the earth
and assist with this my act of magic.'

Trace your line back to the east thus creating a circle around you. Go back to the centre and face east. Stretch out your arms to make a cross, visualise the figures and intone the names at the compass points that you did in the Lesser Banishing Ritual of the Pentagram earlier. Feel them being there strongly, and they will be.

Declare the intention of your work and make a general invocation of divinity such as the invocation that you used earlier, *'Blessed art thou Lord of creation etc'* or some such of your choosing. You are placing your work under the auspices of the most high and this is an acknowledgement of that. To declare your authority to command the success of your magical working you can do no better than to use the Enochian invocation that you used earlier - *'O Sonuf Vaorsagi'* etc - then an invocation of the energies of creation as with the use of the *'I invoke thee thou angels of the celestial spheres'* etc as you have also used earlier. Then will come the summoning of the energies particular to your work be they elemental or planetary, and the work itself will then follow.

At the completion of your working the energies involved will need to be thanked and dismissed with the License to Depart, and then left to it. The ritual is then wound down and you should then dismiss it from your mind. Having dismissed the energies involved use the following as a final act of acknowledgement, *'Non nobis Domini, non nobis etc'* which you have used earlier on in your work. Then will come the banishing and thus the enabling of yourself to return to the everyday.

Use the Lesser Banishing Ritual of the Pentagram, which you are familiar with by now. Alternatively, if working as above, use the relevant banishing pentagram at the appropriate compass point, or the appropriate elemental pentagram for an elemental working. This formula, which I have used over many years, has served me well and can be adapted and used in all manner of magical work and once you have gained proficiency with it, you will no doubt be inspired with your own ideas. I have successfully used it in the making and consecrating of a wide variety of talismans, in candle magics, evocations, invocations, necromancy, the blessing and the cursing of a given situation (or indeed person), working with a particular element as with the use of fluid condensers (see later on) and a host of other schemes, dreams and inspirations. The possibilities are boundless and endless.

CHAPTER FOUR

'The Allies of the Green and the Growing'

Plants have always had an important part to play in our arte; be it in medicine or in magic and it would be foolish to underestimate them, for they are indeed allies as we pass though life. It is important to spend as much time as you can out in the countryside and observe what is happening around you. It would be no bad idea to spend a year studying a hedgerow and taking note of the life therein.

Even in a town there will be the canal or an area that has some plant life thereon. Better still, take an allotment and get your hands dirty. Rejoice in the mud, the wet, the cold biting winds and the merciless heat of the hot summer Sun. Now you really are experiencing the elements! Get to know the plants, their properties, and their capabilities. Find a plant identification book in the library or somewhere, go out and find them, sit amongst them and take note. Plants, like people, are influenced by planetary considerations and will need to be harvested for use in our arte accordingly. If it is not possible to harvest a plant at the best planetary time for it, then aim to harvest at the full Moon when the sap will be more pronounced and thus the life force also. The astrological associations of a plant will vary according to what source you use. I always stick to the 17th century herbalist Culpeper because his classifications work.

Plants such as nettles are obviously of a martial quality and therefore are under the governance of the planet Mars. With that being so then the best time for their harvesting would be the Tuesday before the full Moon. (Tuesday being ruled by Mars)

It is advisable for any bottles or jars that are used for the storage of the allies to be cleansed and dedicated for the work and then kept for nothing else but.

One of the more useful acts of green sorcery is the birthing of the fluid condenser. The Philtre of Empowerment, known as *The Universal Fluid Condenser*' is an indispensable and potent aid to the success of our artes. These magical fluids are extremely useful in talismanic magic and with the working of elemental magics. They can be used for the making of magical mirrors, the supercharging of poppets and the creating of magical servitors and thought forms.

There are several means for their conception and we will use a simple but effective method. The necessary plants will need to be gathered on their appropriate day or, if not then, at the full of the Moon. You will also need a clean and dedicated jar (a kilner jar would do fine) and you will need some alcohol for the preserving of the condenser and the extracting of the essences of the plant spirit. You can use methylated spirit but I'm not that keen on it, you would be better off with a high proof brandy.

The philtre of our arte will also be given extra potency by the addition of Tincture of Gold. This worthy aid is simple to prepare. On a Sunday and on a waxing Moon declare your intentions. Spend a few moments contemplating the energies of the Sun (as gold has strong solar associations) and then heat a piece of gold such as a ring or some such. Place in a clean container say 100 ml or so of clean water (not tap water). When your gold is hot drop it into the water. It will probably splutter so take care. Separate the gold from the water without anything touching the water, to prevent it from becoming contaminated – do this by pouring the water into another container. Reheat the gold and repeat this process five more times making six in all. Strain through a clean cloth and bottle. This is now your tincture of gold, label it as such and keep it away from the profane.

Gather on their respective planetary days the following herbs:

Angelica (Sun), Sage (Jupiter), Lime flowers (Jupiter), Cucumber (Moon), Acacia leaves or blossom (Sun), Chamomile flowers (Sun), Lily flowers or leaves (Moon), Cinnamon (Venus), Nettles (Mars), Peppermint (Venus), Poplar leaves (Saturn), Violet flowers or leaves (Venus), Willow bark or leaves (Moon), Tobacco (Mars), Lavender flowers (Mercury).

At the full of the Moon take equal amounts thereof and place in a clean kilner jar or the like and then cover with either pure alcohol or brandy. You can, for further potency, add some of your own blood or sexual fluids.

Now place this jar somewhere safe and in the dark, away from prying eyes and let it gestate until the next full Moon. It is now brought out into the light of day and allowed to greet the world. Strain through some clean cloth and add to it ten drops of your gold tincture prepared previously. This condenser will last for years and is useful when added to inks or paints when constructing talismans. It can be used to great success in the manufacturing of a poppet by including some of it in the body of the doll. Your magical regalia will be the better for being anointed with some of it and it is also very good when constructing the bodies of elementals that will serve you, or to paint on the back of a picture or mirror for magical work.

It can be placed in a dish and charged with planetary or elemental energies and left to influence a room or a given area. There are many uses for it that will become apparent, as it holds magical energies like a storage battery.

Also there are four elemental philtres that are of use for working with elemental energies. Whilst their method of construction is the same as that which is given above their modus operandi and methods of use are different. Each one will only work for its   element. They are made thus.

Fire:

Contemplate the fiery essence of creation and at a waxing Moon and when the Moon is in a fire sign, such as Aries, Leo or Sagittarius, (check with an ephemeris if you are not sure where the Moon is) then take equal amounts of the following herbs and place them in a clean jar according to our custom: onion, garlic, pepper and mustard (mind your eyes and skin as they are an irritant) and cover as you did before with alcohol or brandy. Seal and place in the dark. Leave for one month and open when the Moon is back in the fire sign that it was in when you began this operation. Strain and add some of your gold tincture. Now bottle and label it clearly, then store it away in the dark somewhere safe.

Water:

Let the Moon be waxing and in a watery sign such as Cancer, Scorpio or Pisces. Being aware of the element water, take equal amounts of the following and cover in our jar with alcohol or brandy: oats, sugar, the petals or leaves of peony and the bark or the leaves of the cherry tree. Let them gestate as our arte demands for one lunar month, until the Moon is back in the sign under which you started this operation. Then strain and add some of your gold tincture after which store in a dark bottle.

Air:

The Moon must be in the air signs of Gemini, Libra or Aquarius. Invoke the element air to acknowledge your act and place in a clean jar as we have done with the other elemental philtres the following herbs: hazel nuts, leaves or bark, rose petals or leaves, juniper berries and coriander seeds. Cover with alcohol and treat as you have done with the others.

Earth:

Here we will need the Moon to be in one of the earthy signs of Taurus, Virgo or Capricorn. Call upon the earth to witness and assist then place equal amounts of parsley root, leaves or seeds, caraway seed, plantain leaves, lemon balm and carnation flowers (the latter will be better for our work if they are not a modern hybrid) in our jar as with the others. Again cover with alcohol. After the lunar month when the Moon is back in the sign where you started, strain and add some of the gold tincture, then store somewhere safe. To all these philtres you may add some of your life force.

These elemental philtres will keep for years and will stand by you in good stead. They can be used to effect workings in keeping with each element on various levels, and are not solely bound to the world of the mundane. You will only need to use a few drops at a time.

The areas of elemental influence are as follows:

Fire:

Where acts of assertion are required be they cursing and destructive or protective. This is very good for creating a servant for guarding something or improving one's maleness; also for powers of creativity.

Water:

Use for all acts of love and friendship; also for joy, fertility or psychic receptivity.

Air:

Healing, travel and learning. The mental realms and matters relating to the mind; also for dispersing someone or something getting them to move on. Will promote bickering and arguments between people.

Earth:

Money or employment. Gaining a house to live in. Growing things. Blocking something or someone. Improving a business or destroying one.

When working with an element, if you are working for a positive end work on the waxing Moon, for a negative outcome work on a waning Moon. It will be pertinent to work also when the Moon is in the relevant elemental sign. There are several ways in which the elemental energies can be harnessed to your will. We will look at two of them. The first is the simplest which doesn't mean that it is the least effective.

Contemplate the elemental energy that you wish to work with. For the fire element take a clean piece of paper and write down that which you want to happen clearly and in an unambiguous manner.

Now, saying:

> *'Hear me O element fire for this charge I lay, thou art subject*
> *unto my will in every way.*
> *Hear my words addressed to thee, for this my will*
> *So Mote It Be!'*

Trace in the air above your piece of paper the invoking pentagram of fire and pour on to it several drops of the fire element philtre. Then look into the paper and see your will being accomplished; burn it in an open flame and again see your will coming to pass. Believe it and know it. Now forget it and it will come to birth.

Such magic will come to pass within the lunar month but for some problems that are stubborn, more than one working may be required, but that will depend on how much energy you raise.

To work with the water element, take in your chalice some water, though not tap water. Water from a lake, river or spring will be ideal. Dwell upon the properties of the element water and drop into the chalice several drops of your water element philtre and declare your intent.

Now trace over the chalice the invoking pentagram of water, saying:

'Hear me O element water for this charge I lay etc'

See in the water that which you would occur. Now throw the water into a stream or lake or such like and see your magic happening as you would will.

The air element works on the application of evaporation and can be performed thus. Filling yourself with the feeling of the element air and as with the other elemental workings, say what you are about. Then taking again a small amount of water and adding to it some of the air element philtre; pour it into a metal dish or something that can withstand heat and place it on an open flame.

Trace over it the invoking pentagram of air saying as you do:

'Hear me O element air for this charge I lay etc'

Looking into the rising steam see your will being made true in the world. Know that that which you see in the steam will come to pass, for it is this firm conviction, this unassailable will that will see it brought to being; there can be no other outcome.

With the earth we need to gather some soil from each of the four compass points. Mix them together and then place some on a dish. Your pentacle will be ideal. Contemplate and summon the earth element. Pour on to the earth before you in your dish or pentacle some of the earth elemental philtre. Trace over it the invoking pentagram of earth saying:

'Hear me O element earth for this charge I lay etc'.

Look deeply into the earth before you and see that which you would come to pass. Know that it is true. Release the element back to whence it came and let it do its work.

These are simple spell formulas which can be adapted and worked more elaborately should you so wish, although that doesn't guarantee greater success. For example each elemental working given above can easily be worked within a ritual framework such as that which you have used for the consecrating of your magical regalia.

This in itself is useful for gaining the *'flow of ritual'* and promoting your sense of magical being.

Another method of working with this system is with the use of geomantic symbology. Geomancy is an ancient but potent system of divination, and from its sixteen symbols can be evolved a series of sigils which can and are used within the arte of talismanic magic. They can also be combined with this work. When working with the fire element, for example, take those symbols that are appropriate to the work such as, if it is a positive piece of magic regarding the fire element, the symbols of Fortuna Major. For negative fire workings you would use Cauda Draconis. Draw the symbols on your paper with intent, following the now-established pattern, and burn to release the energy.

With earth the paper could be buried and as it rotted the magic would come to pass. For the water element, let a stream or river carry it away and for the air stand on a high point in the breeze and throw it into the air and let the winds carry it away to fruition.

The Geomantic Symbols:

PUER: Fire

SIGILS OF PUER:

AMISSIO: Earth

SIGILS OF AMISSIO:

ALBUS: Air

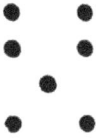

SIGILS OF ALBUS:

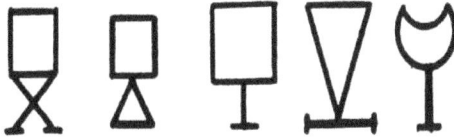

POPULUS: Water

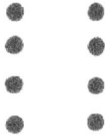

SIGILS OF POPULUS:

FORTUNA MAJOR: Fire

SIGILS OF FORTUNA MAJOR:

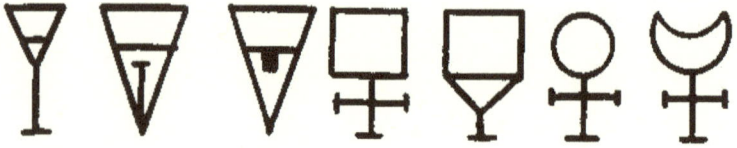

CONJUNCTIO: Earth

SIGILS OF CONJUNCTIO:

PUELLA: Water

SIGILS OF PUELLA:

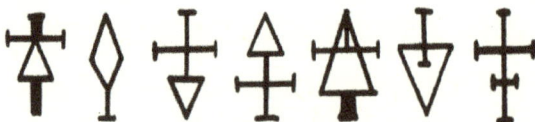

RUBEUS: Water

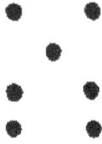

SIGILS OF RUBEUS:

ACQUISITIO: Fire

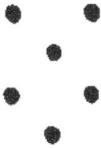

SIGILS OF ACQUISITIO:

CARCER: Earth

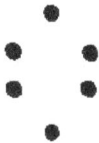

SIGILS OF CARCER:

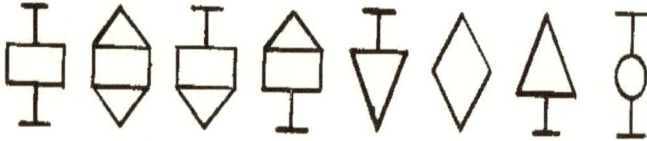

TRISTITIA: Air

SIGILS OF TRISTIIA:

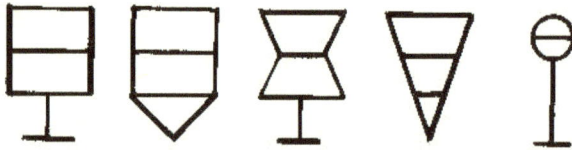

LAETITIA: Water

SIGILS OF LAETITIA:

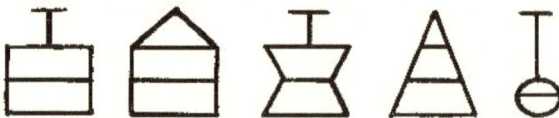

CAPUT DRACONIS: Fire

SIGILS OF CAPUT DRACONIS:

CAUDA DRACONIS: Earth

SIGILS OF CAUDA DRACONIS:

FORTUNA MINOR: Air

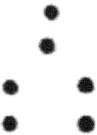

SIGILS OF FORTUNA MINOR:

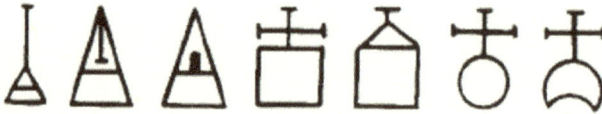

VIA: Water

SIGILS OF VIA:

Whilst this is not a herbal in the sense of making the sick and the lame well and enabling the halt to walk (such skills are amply covered elsewhere) this work does however deal with other interesting uses of plants, that tradition and indeed experience have shown can be used to treat conditions of the body that are not in the realms of the physician. How often has the sorcerer/ess in times past been approached for philtres to promote love or lust, or poisons to remove individuals that are in their way? Naturally the use of death-dealing plants, for legal reasons, cannot be covered here. Probably the most successful practitioner of such artes was the 17th century French woman Catherine Deyshayes, known as La Voisin, who started her career as a compiler of herbal simples and beauty creams based on arsenic which were in great demand by the general populus. However, having gone as high as one can go as an abortionist, herbalist and the unofficial sorceress to the nobility, including the mistress of the king, she eventually fell foul of the law owing no doubt to the fact that she knew too much about too many people. But for you the knowledge of simple philtres will suffice.

To give one example, traditionally, the African tree Yohimbe contains various interesting properties that have a strong erectile effect on male genitalia. Whilst there are several observances and methods of preparation to access the amazing powers of this plant, which makes Viagra look like smarties, the easiest way is to use a homeopathic mother tincture and take a few drops in a glass of water. This could be appropriately charged with a martial current via ritual for a more subtle effect, but if not the effects can be greatly enhanced if you drink plenty of orange juice as the vitamin C will also magnify the effects.

Other green allies that will aid and promote lust are Saw Palmetto, again as a homeopathic mother tincture useful for males (also instrumental in treating benign swelling of the prostate gland).

Damiana is a superb herb of choice that works more on the magical levels to promote attraction from the opposite sex and of course, homoeopathically supercharging your pheromones. This again is simple to prepare. Take a clean never been used glass jar and on a Friday (the day of Venus and fleshly delights) place within it a cotton wool swab of your sweat, taken from around your genitalia and armpit. Place this in the jar with some very clean water, not tap nor rain water. Now as the homeopaths do, it must be potentised. To do this, bang the jar on a hard surface one hundred times; not breaking the jar of course. Having done this, throw the water away and refill and repeat. This must be done forty-nine times. Why? As the homeopaths will repeat such an operation six times for a physical effect on the body, they will also repeat this technique sometimes into the hundreds or thousands of times to produce something that will work on very deep levels.

For this work the potentising operation will need to be repeated until you have performed forty-nine dilutions and potentisations, forty-nine being 7 x 7. Seven is the number of Venus. This could be easily accompanied by burning a little Venusian incense, such as a good quality musk oil; more so if you can mix in a little ambergris oil. The concentration on Venusian imagery will be of great worth and so will simple chants relevant to the intent of your work. Bottle and store safely and use on your pulse points sparingly. Whilst this will attract the opposite sex to you as they are picking up on the lure of the pheromones which will have an effect on their inner responses, other males may feel uncomfortable in your presence and will not know why.

Naturally this simple but effective method of a personalised attraction philtre can be greatly magnified by the use of ritual methods. Other philtres can be made according to the traditions of our arte. On a Friday deck your altar with roses if available and light a green candle, burn also a little Venusian incense. Having recited an invocation to the powers of Venus for the success of the work, place in your chalice a little of the following dried herbs: leaves of vervain, mistletoe berries and the petals or seeds of elecampane. Trace the sigil of Venus in green over the chalice and its contents declaring your intent.

See that which you want to happen, happening therein and declaring

> 'By this act I draw x and y together in the bonds of love and lust'.

The philtre must be strained and stored safely. All that is now needed is for it to be introduced into the presence of the intended. For that their drink will suffice, with one drop placed therein, or, failing that, a few drops on their clothing or seat. The magic will then be released as the philtre becomes the carrier of the intention. Other plants of use for the preparation of lustful philtres are the flowers of clary sage, periwinkle, basil, blackberry and chicory. Take, at the full of the Moon, small but equal amounts of cinnamon, vanilla and clary sage; add to this twice the amount of rose petals and twice the amount again of damiana. Place in a clean and dedicated vessel and cover with brandy. Let it steep in the dark for one whole lunar month.

Press out the herbs and collect all the fluid into another jar. Place the herbal remains in another clean jar and cover with clean water. Let it steep for one week, then strain and to this tincture add a little honey, warming up the herbed waters so that the honey melts. Now it can be added to the tincture that you have saved and is in your other clean jar. Let it stand undisturbed for another week then strain, bottle and store safely for at least a month before use. A teaspoonful in a glass of water or some such, over which an invocation of lust has been recited, will promote pleasingly such activities.

One of the least known but highly effective methods of working with a plant spirit is in the birthing of an alruan or the magistellus 'The little master'. These creatures are excellent as guards to places or people and are brought into being quite easily if you have a little patience and determination.

There are to my knowledge two very good ways of setting about this work. One is by carving a figure from the branch of the rowan tree and the other is hunting down a mandrake. We will explore both methods as their aims and methods to bring them into being are similar. Sometime near the full of the Moon and between the shortest day and the spring equinox hunt down your mandrake.

Mandrakes will grow in Britain but do not like wet winters, so if you cannot find one then you must use the root of the English mandrake, *bryonia dioicia*. Do not ingest either of these plants and wash your hands after use. These plants can have big roots and we will need a means to dig them up. I would suggest that you use your black-handled knife for this. At night and in secret go to the mandrake and explain to the plant what you are about. Without being observed by anyone, draw a circle with the knife of the arte around it. Slowly and carefully remove the soil from around the plant root and ease it out gently. Do not let it touch the ground as its powers will leak back into the soil.

Now you must leave something for the payment of the plant, perhaps a coin or some grain or even some of your life blood. But whatever it is that you do, cut off the top inch or so of the plant and replant it. Hide the root about your being and scurry home without talking if possible. Now you must carve the root into a figure of the opposite sex to yourself and ask the spirit to guard the home or person that it is required for. To ensure that the maximum potency of the spirit is present bury the little master in the soil in a church yard or at a crossroads, failing that your garden.

Now for the next lunar month you must regularly and without fail water the plant with a mixture of water and milk to which a few drops of your blood have been added. At the end of the lunar month dig up the root and clean it, now it has to be censed and dried off. The scars from the carving will have healed over and the little master will look very human - more so than some real ones! Daily for the next lunar month, burn a little lemon balm and pass it through the smoke thereof and having instructed the magistellus in its ways and duties, place it near the centre of the home and let it do its work.

An alraun is very similar. To bring one into being you must find a rowan tree and select a branch suitable for carving. As you did with the mandrake, you must prepare this at the same time of the year and lunar cycle. For the next lunar month you will need to water the tree with the same mixture as you did the mandrake; declaring your intentions. At the end of the lunar month, without being seen, cut the previously selected branch and leave something for payment.

Take it home and carve it into a figure that is the opposite sex to you and treat it as you did the mandrake; although you will not need to bury it. When either the alruan or the mandrake are completed and prior to them going into action, they must spend the night in your bed and as the old tradition says *'They must be known for the night as your wife'*.

An herb garden if you have space will be of paramount importance. The growing and harvesting of plants will be a magical act in itself. Simply spending time among them is beneficial to one's well-being and should not be underestimated by any one.

A good and traditional aspergillum for the sprinkling of the holy waters about one's place of working, thus promoting a sense of being within a sacred space, is created by gathering the following herbs at the approach of the full Moon and tying them together with some clean thread. Take the following from your herb garden: hyssop, vervain, valerian, mint, basil, fennel, rosemary, lavender and sage. These herbs will be found very effective for the dispersing of disquieting energies. Or, failing the collecting of the above, a simple sprig of hyssop will suffice.

Hyssop is also good to add to any baths that you are taking, to prepare yourself for any magical acts. So is loosestrife, which as its name suggests, will quiet disturbed environments. This was a highly esteemed herb of the early English sorcerers and should, in my view, be more widely used than it is today.

It is important that you approach the plants that you are going to harvest with respect. Talk to the plant, tell them what you're about and take no more than is necessary.

Traditionally there has been a strong input into herbology from astrology, with Culpeper declaring that astrologers were the only fit people to study medicine. This might sound quaint or just crazy, but there are good reasons for acknowledging astrological considerations in gathering your herbs for your work. There are, according to the traditions of our arte, various rules and observances to consider when harvesting herbs for magic which I list here. You will find that they'll enhance your magical workings considerably when taken into consideration. If you have no or little knowledge of astrology, then learn. A sorcerer/ess worthy of their salt ought to be able to cast a chart. There are many books about that will teach you the basics. Some do it better than others, so don't despair if you pick up a work that is less than clear. Keep learning.

In casting a chart for the moment when you are planning to pick your herb consider the following:

- Fortify the nature of the herb or herbs with the lord of the Ascendant. In other words let the planet that rules the ascendant for the time that you are going to pick your herb be in a favourable position to the planet that rules the herb of your picking. That is, do not pick if they be in opposition or square (180 and 90 degrees respectively) to the planet that rules the herb of your working.

- Let the lord of the tenth be strong. That is, if the planet that rules the tenth house of the chart cast is weak, such as if it is retrograde or making a bad aspect to the malefics such as Mars and Saturn, or in its fall or detriment, then it is not strong. Then let it be placed where it is favoured. If it is the Moon who rules the tenth then there are other considerations that will make it weak. Try to make sure that the planet that rules the tenth is at least not weak, and is preferably in a favourable position to the Sun, Jupiter or Venus. Better still if the planet of the tenth is in its dignity or in its exaltation.

- Fortify the Moon, Sun and ascendant. In other words let the Sun and the Moon be in good houses, preferably their own or in houses that they have some dignity in, or, better still are exalted therein.

- Do not let them be in ill-dignified houses where they have their detriment.

- Furthermore, these two planets must not be ill-favoured by Mars or Saturn. Let the planet that governs the ascendant be free from being retrograde or being in its fall or detriment.

- Make sure that the planet is at least 17 degrees away from the Sun, although if it is within ½ degree that will be good. In old astrological thinking if a planet was within 17 degrees of the Sun, then it was considered that the Sun was having a negative impact on the planet and stopping it from acting according to its nature. This was called 'under the sunbeams'. Although when making an exact conjunction, as at ½ degree, this was considered to strengthen the planet.

The Moon is considered weak when:

- It is less than 12 degrees from the Sun, referred to as being combust. This aspect is worse when the Moon is applying to the Sun than when it is leaving.

- It is in Scorpio particularly at its fall at 3 degrees. Furthermore, if the Moon is making either a conjunction, square or opposition to a malefic then this does not bode well for the harvesting.

- It is in its detriment or fall.

- It is void, that is forming no aspects at all to any planet.

Although much of the above may seem hard to comply with, and perhaps unnecessary, you would do well to follow as much as you can when gathering herbs for magical work. At least let the planet that governs the herb be free from the bad influence of malefic planets. However if you are gathering herbs of a saturnine or martial nature for malefic working, then they will need to be gathered on a waning Moon and will be better if they can be harvested in the last few days of the last quarter of the Moon. At the end of the day it is your will that makes the magic come to pass; all that the above considerations do is help speed it on to realisation.

CHAPTER FIVE

'Bending the bendable'

Nottingham's first law of magic is to remember that you are not God and with your magics - you are attempting to *Bend the bendable'*. There are some things that can't be done, although, having said that, there is an awful lot that can.

Nottingham's second law of magic is to be mindful of what you work for, because will it be what you want when you get it? There are many methods of spellworking and the seasoned sorcerer/ess will no doubt come up with a few of their own as time goes by.

One of the big areas that you will need to be adept at is the constructing and hallowing of talismans. Talismans are more than a psychological prop: they can be charged with an energy that works and will bring the desired result even when the individual that it has been made for is in ignorance of its existence.

Whilst many talismanic designs abound, there appears to be very little good information about regarding the hallowing and empowering of the charm. There are several methods that work, some simple, some complex.

Of all the techniques that work and work well the Middle Pillar method is extremely useful, not only for this work but in many other magical operations. The Middle Pillar working is from the Kabbalah and therefore you will need to have a working knowledge of its mysteries to make sense of some of its more subtle points.

The Kabbalah is the backbone of the Western Magical Tradition although others may want to disagree. Whilst this is not the place to go into details of Kabalistic teachings some simple explanation of the more salient features are called for. See this work's companion volume *Otz Chim* for more details. Out of nothing came everything and divinity became aware of itself. The expressions thereof are demonstrated by a glyph known as the *'Tree of Life'*. This has both a dark as well as a light side to it. We can see this being manifested in both our own natures and that of the godhead. When does good become bad?

If we grant mercy we may consider it a fine thing to do but do it too much and it becomes a weakness promoting an undesirable outcome. Who defines good and who will define bad? We must make our own judgments, which is part of taking responsibility for ourselves and our own actions. It is a mark of our maturity and the development of our own individuality to do so. As Jung would say, *'It is an expression of the individuation process.'*

The first manifestation according to the tradition is that of Kether, meaning The Crown. This sphere is one of pure spirit and can only be understood by us by the use of symbols and imagery. The next manifestation of this is Chokmah, pronounced Hokma, meaning Wisdom and is seen as male, its imagery and incenses are such. The third manifestation is Binah, meaning Understanding and is seen as female. It has much in the way of saturnine associations and such imagery is accredited to it.

The fourth stage of manifestation is Chesed pronounced Hesed, which means Mercy. Jupiter and its associations are pronounced here. Fifthly we have Geburah meaning Strength with all the attributes of Mars. Sixthly is the Sun at Tiphereth, meaning Beauty and with its solar considerations. Seventh is Netzach meaning Victory, which is also associated with Venus and the relevant attributes thereof. From which flows Hod the eighth sphere of manifestation whose meaning is Glory and has the potencies of Mercury. This leads on to the ninth sphere of Yesod, foundation, the sphere of the Moon and all its concerns and finally Malkuth, the Earth, the everyday world that we inhabit.

Each sphere, or Sephira as they are known, has a God name and image which the rest of the energy is subservient to. There is a definite chain of command, which must be invoked in due order. After the God name comes the Archangel, once again with its own name and imagery, then the order of angels and then the energies' physical manifestation, such as the relevant planet. The planetary spirits will also be governed by this scheme. All the spheres have a wide association of ideas, imagery and powers which we can use for the successful practice of our arte. They all have their own incenses and colours, sounds, symbols and sigils.

The Middle Pillar exercise, which is very potent for our work, is based on the middle spheres of the tree. Standing upright (although some authorities say lie down or sit upright) empty your mind and relax your muscles. Concentrate on the area above your head, see above you a brilliant gleaming sphere that glows and radiates energy. Consider this to be Kether, the Crown.

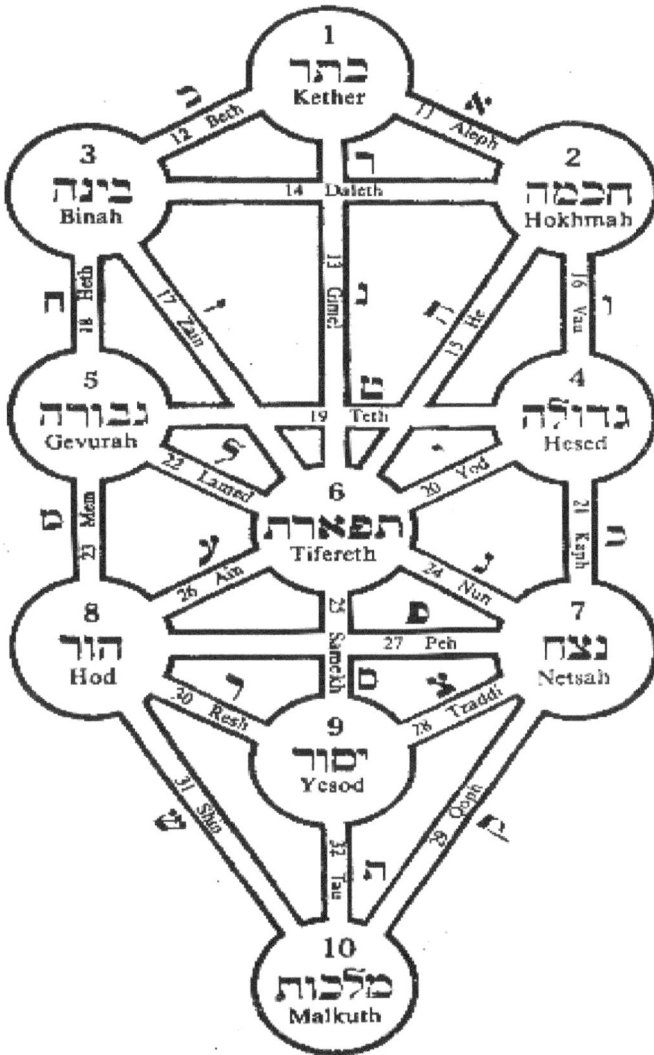

The Tree of Life

Try to place, as best you can, your consciousness into this glowing sphere and intone the word EHIEH, pronounced as eh-heh-yeh, meaning, *'I am.'* This is the god name governing the energies of Kether. Visualise a shaft of this energy flowing through you to reach your throat where it blossoms into a lavender sphere. Again endeavour to place your consciousness into it and the god name is 'YHVH ELOHIM', yod-heh-vav-heh-el-o-him, *'Lord God.'*

Bring the light down to your heart region and see it blossom into a golden sphere. As before, place your consciousness into it and intone the God name 'YHVH ALOAH VA DAATH', yod-heh-vav-heh-el-oah-va-daath, meaning, *'God made manifest in the sphere of the mind.'*

See the energies flow down to the genital region and let them blossom as a purple sphere. Placing your consciousness again into the sphere intone 'SHADDAI EL CHAI', shad-dia-el-chay, *'Almighty living God.'*

Now concentrate on your feet and bring the energy down to them. See a black sphere form here and again be in there. The God name to be intoned for this sphere is 'ADONAI HA ARETZ' Adoni-ha-aretz, *'Lord of this Earth'.*

Having now established the spheres of the middle pillar you will probably have felt a distinct sensation at each station. Sometimes this can be felt as warmth or a tingling sense, it will vary to each individual but you will feel something, even if it is a greater awareness of yourself at this region.

Having reached Malkuth at your feet, go back to the top sphere Kether. Now as you breathe out let the energies flow down the left side of your body to the Malkuth sphere at your feet. Here pause and now bring them up your right side, on your in-breath, back to the top where you started, forming a complete circuit. Do this several times and then perform the same operation down the front of your body to your feet, then to the top of your head via the back of your body. When completed, flood your aura with the colour of the working and intone the God name several times. Feel the energies invoked stir within you. Let everyday awareness pass you by and be the energy invoked. This may seem complicated but practice daily with this formula will bring success. If you do practice daily - and it would be no bad thing so to do - flood your aura with a brilliant light and impose upon it a sense of well-being.

Do not under-estimate this Middle Pillar technique because it is one of the keys to successful magic and we will use it a lot. The subtle energies that flow throughout creation can be connected with via the schema of astrology, which is why astrology is important to the sorcerer/ess.

The astrological classification of incense, colour or desires is something that we will be working with a lot. Therefore I give an astrological table of classification below. A more detailed account can be found in Crowley's *777*. Whilst there are various accounts of such information in print these days, some of it I would consider suspect and in keeping with an all too common airy-fairy approach to magic that currently is so popular.

Whilst it is a good thing for you to construct your own invocations I also include under each planetary heading invocations that, because of their age and long use, do have, I think, a power of their own which will definitely add that something to your magic.

SATURN:

Saturn is the planet of Binah and is considered to be a dark stern planet, which is seen as a disciplinarian and an energy of restraint and restriction. However, it is also associated with agriculture, buildings, old people and karmic activity, death, wills and debts. Its colour is black and incense is myrrh. Its oil is civet and number is three. The metal lead, and the jewel jet, are also attributed to Saturn. Saturn's magical image is a tall dark mature woman seen against a backdrop of the night sky that has flashes of crimson running through it with the sea beneath.

God Name, YHVH ELOHIM; Archangel, Tzaphkiel; Order of Angels, Aralim; Intelligence, Agiel; Spirit, Zazel; Olympic Spirit, Aratron; Archdemon, Lucifuge Rofacale (not Lucifer the Star of the Morning); Order of Demons, The Sateriel, the Concealers; Virtue silence; Vice inertia.

Planetary Square:

4	9	2
3	5	7
8	1	6

Seal of Planet:

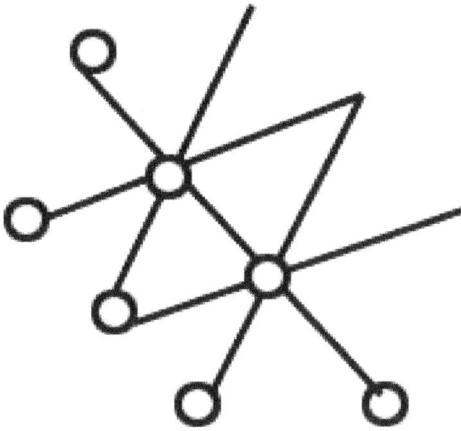

Sigil of Intelligence: Sigil of Spirit:

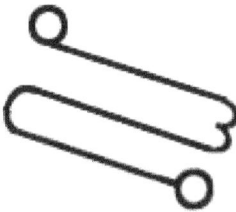

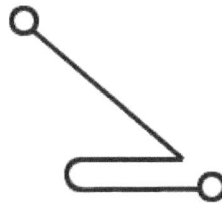

Sigil of Olympic Spirit:

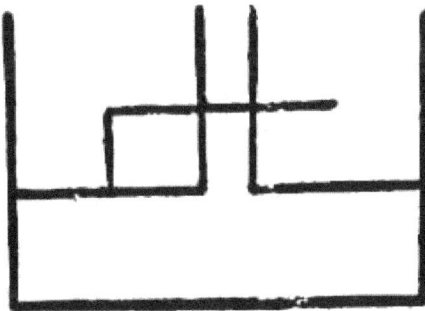

Invocation for Saturn:

'Hear me O ye divine forces of Shabbati!
For in and by that mighty and potent name YHVH ELOHIM
and by the name of the Holy Archangel Tzaphkiel
and by the might of the Aralim do I invocate thee this day.
Come forth out of your gloomy solitude ye Saturnine spirits,
come with your cohorts, come with diligence to the place
where I am going to begin my operation; be ye attentive
unto my labours and assist me with this my holy act of
magic.
For I invoke thee by the mighty name YHVH ELOHIM!'

'Coniuro vos Shabbati.
Coniuro in nomine YHVH ELOHIM et in nomine archangeli
Tzaphkiel
et per Aralim sanctos.
Adiuvate nunc!'

JUPITER:

This planet of Chesed is benevolent and expansive. Its energies are those of good luck and abundance, spirituality and visions, long journeys and church matters. Also associated are bankers, money gain and legal concerns. Its colour is blue and incense and oil is cedar. Its number is four and jewel is amethyst. Its metal is tin. Jupiter's magical image is a crowned and kingly figure enthroned, dressed in robes of deep blue with orange running through.

God name, EL; Archangel, Tzadkiel; Order of Angels, Chashmalim; Intelligence, Yophiel; Spirit, Hismael; Olympic Spirit, Bethor; Archdemon, Astaroth; Order of Demons, Gamchicoth ,the disturbers of souls; Virtue mercy; Vice gluttony.

Planetary Square:

4	14	15	1
9	7	6	12
5	11	10	8
16	2	3	13

Seal of Planet:

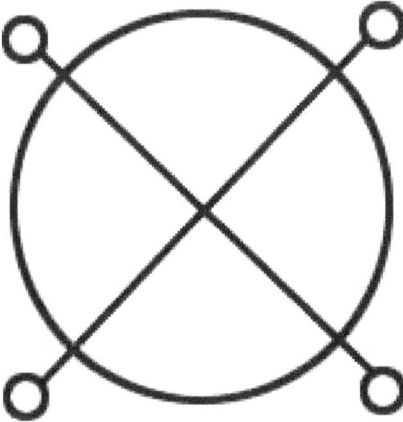

Sigil of Intelligence:

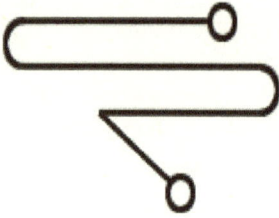

Sigil of Spirit:

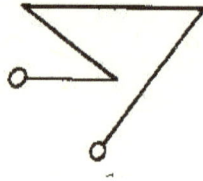

Sigil of Olympic Spirit:

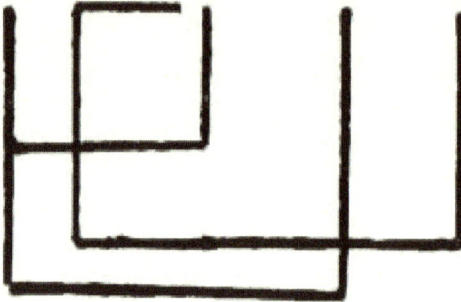

Invocations of Jupiter:

'O ye divine energies of Tzadek.
Ye holy ones of giving.
Hear me for I do invoke thee by the mighty and potent
name EL! and by the Holy Archangel Tzadkiel
and by the might of the Chashmalim.
Therefore come thou speedily O ye spirits who preside over
the operations of this day,
hasten to my assistance and be propitious to my
undertakings.
Assist me now with this my holy act of magic. By the potent
name EL divine and wonderful!'

'Coniuro vos Tzadek!
Coniuro in nomine EL magna!
Et in nomine archangeli Tzadkiel et per Chasmalim sanctos.
Adiuvate nunc!

MARS:

This planet is associated with Geburah and its energies are assertive, they can also be destructive. Mars has always been associated with war and times when extra strength is needed. It is good for protection as well as attack. There was a time when the planet was associated with agriculture. It is also associated with an increase in fertility and is good to promote masculinity. Its colour is red and five is its number. Its incense is dragon's blood or pepper and its metal is iron. The oil is opopanax and the jewel is ruby. Mars' magical image is a tall and strong king, an armed and mighty figure dressed with armour, over which is worn red robes. Within the red fabric there are flashes of green.

God name, ELOHIM GIBOR; Archangel, Khamael; Order of Angels, Seraphim; Intelligence, Graphiel; Spirit, Bartzabel; Olympic Spirit, Phaleg; Archdemon, Asmodeus; Order of Demons, Golachab, the Incendiaries; Virtue Courage; Vice Cruelty.

Planetary Square:

11	24	7	20	3
4	12	25	8	16
17	5	13	21	9
10	18	1	14	22
23	6	19	2	15

Seal of Planet:

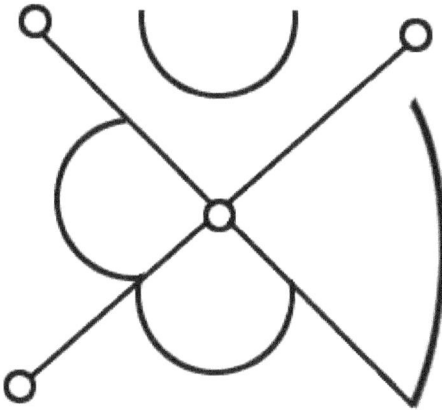

Sigil of Intelligence:

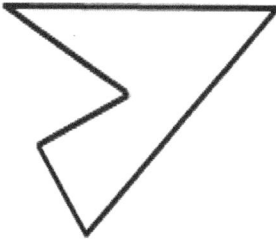

Sigil of Spirit:

Sigil of Olympic Spirit:

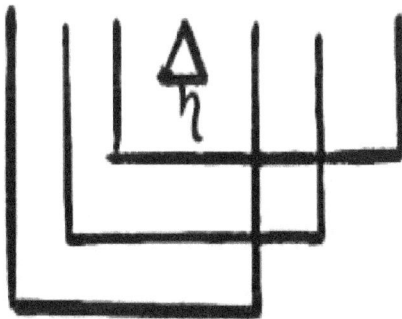

Invocations of Mars:

'Hear me O ye mighty energies of Madim! Hear me!
For thee I do invoke this day by the mighty and the potent
name ELOHIM GIBOR!
That name which thine energies obey!
And by the Holy Archangel Khamael and the might of the
Seraphim do I invoke thee O Madim! Therefore come O thou
powers of the red planet!
Come forth I command and assist me in this my holy act of
magic!
By the name and power of ELOHIM GIBOR!'

'Coniuro vos Madim!
Conjuro in Domini ELOHIM GIBOR omnipotentens!
Et in Domini archangeli Khamael et per seraphim sanctos.
Adiuvate nunc!'

SUN:

This planet is attributed to Tiphereth and has the powers of promoting health and well-being, prosperity and riches, also the favour and friendship of important people. It promotes power, success and victory. Sol Invicto! The unconquerable Sun! Its colour is gold, as is its' metal. Its jewel is the tiger eye. The incense and oil is olibanum (frankincense) and its number is six. Its imagery is the crowned and throned king dressed in gold and white, sitting in sunlight.

God name, YHVH ALOAH VA DAATH; Archangel, Mikael; Order of Angels, Malakim; Intelligence, Nakhiel; Spirit, Sorath; Olympic Spirit, Och; Archdemon, Belphegor; Order of Demons, Tagahrim, the disputers; Virtue Harmony; Vice pride.

Planetary Square:

6	32	3	34	35	1
7	11	27	28	8	30
19	14	16	15	23	24
18	20	22	21	17	13
25	29	10	9	26	12
36	5	33	4	2	31

Seal of Planet:

Sigil of Intelligence:

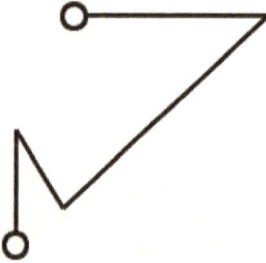

Sigil of Spirit:

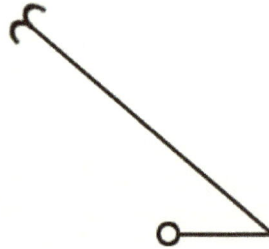

Sigil of Olympic Spirit:

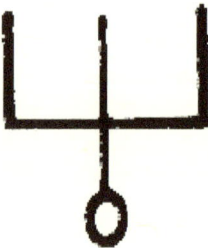

Invocations of the Sun:
'Hear me O thou royal powers of Shemesh, hear me!
For I do this day invoke thee
by the mighty and potent name YHVH ALOAH VA DAATH!
God made manifest in the sphere of the mind!
Furthermore do I invoke thee by the power of the Holy Archangel Mikael and by the might of the Malakim, O thou glorious power of Shemesh! Aid me!
For thee I do invoke in the mighty name YHVH ALOAH VA DAATH!'

'Coniuro vos Shemesh!
Coniuro in nomine YHVH ALOAH VA DAATH!
Et in nomine archangelos Mikael omnipotens et per melekim sanctum.
Adiuvate nunc!'

VENUS:

This planet equates with Netzach. Its energies are of lust, love and romance. It is good for friendships and the dissolving of hostilities. It also promotes good luck, and anything to do with women is favoured by this planet. Its jewel is the emerald and its colour is green. Roses are also associated with this energy. The incenses and the oils are rose, musk or ambergris. Venus' magical image is a beautiful naked woman bearing lilies and roses, accompanied by doves.

God name, YHVH TZABAOTH; Archangel, Haniel; Order of Angels, Elohim; Intelligence, Hagiel; Spirit, Kedemel; Olympic Spirit, Hagith; Archdemon, Bael; Order of Demons, Hareb Serapel, the Ravens of Death; Virtue love; Vice lust.

Planetary Square:

22	47	16	41	10	35	4
5	23	48	17	42	11	29
30	6	24	49	18	36	12
13	31	7	25	43	19	37
38	14	32	1	26	44	20
21	39	8	33	2	27	45
46	15	40	9	34	3	28

Seal of Planet:

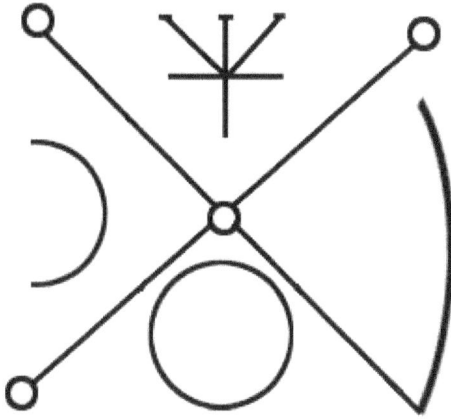

Sigil of Intelligence:

Sigil of Spirit:

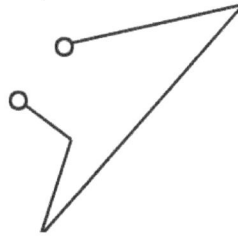

Sigil of Olympic Spirit:

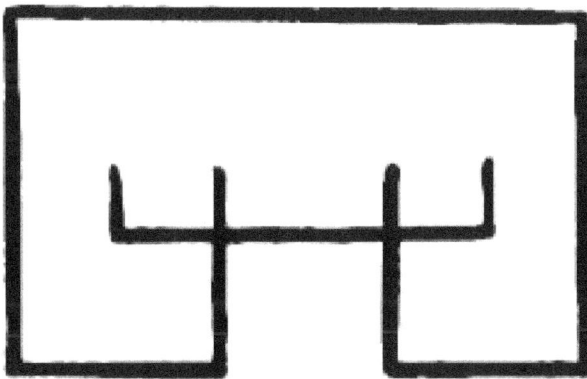

Invocations of Venus:

'Hear me Nogah, O thou holy powers of love and friendship, Hear me!
For I do solemnly invoke thee this day
by the mighty and potent name YHVH Tzabaoth, Lord of armies!
And by the power of the holy archangel Haniel and by the might of the Elohim.
Lend me thine aid, with this my holy act of magic, by the name YHVH TZABAOTH!'

'Coniuro vos Nogah!
Coniuro in Domine YHVH TZABAOTH!
Et in Domine archangelos omnipotens!
Et per Elohim sancti.
Adiuvate nunc!'

MERCURY:

Mercury, the messenger of the Gods, is attributed to Hod and has the powers of communication and learning, selling things or stealing them. This is the energy of successful travel and also of healing. Being the divine trickster Mercury can sometimes be a little unpredictable. Its number is eight and its colour orange. Storax is its incense, although some think that this is too heavy for Mercury and suggest lavender, mastic or mace. The oil is lavender. The jewel is the opal and the metal is mercury although aluminium is safer and easier to work with. Its number is eight. Traditional imagery is the hermaphrodite. Mercury's magical image is the the winged hermaphrodite that carries a staff. The robes are of orange through which runneth purple threads.

God Name, ELOHIM TZABAOTH; Archangel, Raphael; Order of Angels, Beni Elohim; Intelligence, Tiriel; Spirit, Taphthartharath; Olympic Spirit, Ophiel; Archdemon, Adramelech; Order of Demons, Sarhael; Virtue Truthfulness; Vice Falsehood.

Planetary Square:

8	58	59	5	4	62	63	1
49	15	14	52	53	11	10	56
41	23	22	44	45	19	18	48
32	34	35	29	28	38	39	25
40	26	27	37	36	30	31	33
17	47	46	20	21	43	42	24
9	55	54	12	13	51	50	16
64	2	3	61	60	6	7	57

Seal of Planet:

Sigil of Intelligence:

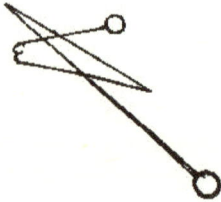

Sigil of Spirit:

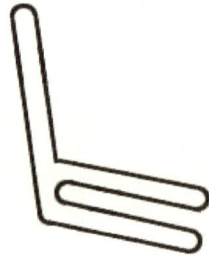

Sigil of Olympic Spirit:

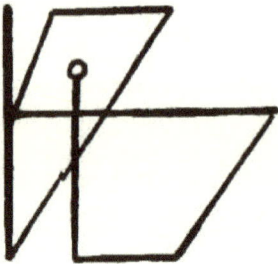

Invocations of Mercury:

'Come speedily O thou powers of Kokab!
Come forth!
For thee I do invoke this day by the mighty and potent name
ELOHIM TZABAOTH!
Furthermore I do invoke thee
in the name of the powerful archangel Raphael and by the
mighty Beni Elohim!
To assist me with this my holy act of magic
By the name Elohim Tzabaoth!'

'Coniuro vos Kokab!
Coniuro in nomine ELOHIM TZABAOTH!
Et in nomine archangelos Raphael!
Et per Beni Elohim sancti!
Adiuvate nunc!'

MOON:

Whilst Luna is considered feminine, in some cosmologies the Moon is regarded as male, and is attributed to Yesod. The Moon is reflective and receptive; she governs her own kingdoms of ebb and flow and therefore can effect growth of all kinds. She is influential in all matters relating to women and to water, and she helps or hinders long journeys. The Moon is good for works of divination and the increasing of one's psychic sensitivities. She is favourable to women in childbirth. She will also promote fertility. The colours of the Moon are purple, silver and white. Nine is her number with her jewel being the pearl. The metal associated with the Moon is obviously silver and the incense is white sandal and camphor. The oil is jasmine.

The Moon's magical image is a large naked, strong and hairy man. This may seem odd considering the female attributes of this planet: it would be well to ponder on this as an image of lunar/Yesod, as these are the subtle energies that have to be effected for anything, regardless of what it is, to be able to manifest on this level. Therefore these realms really do hold up this one and therefore the strong man imagery is highly appropriate. Rather like Atlas carrying the world on his back.

God name, SHADDAI EL CHAI; Archangel, Gabriel; Order of Angels, Kerubim; Intelligence, Malka be-Tarshishim ve-ad Be-Ruachoth Shechalim; Spirit, Chasmodai; Olympic Spirit, Phul; Archdemon, Lilith; Order of Demons, Gamaliel the Obscene Ones; Virtue independence; Vice idleness.

Planetary Square:

37	78	29	70	21	62	13	54	5
6	38	79	30	71	22	63	14	46
47	7	39	80	31	72	23	55	15
16	48	8	40	81	32	64	24	56
57	17	49	9	41	73	33	65	25
26	58	18	50	1	42	74	34	66
67	27	59	10	51	2	43	75	35
36	68	19	60	11	52	3	44	76
77	28	69	20	61	12	53	4	45

Planetary Seal:

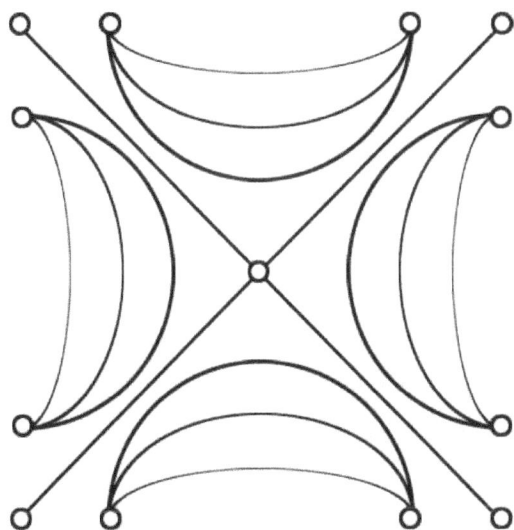

Sigil of Intelligence:

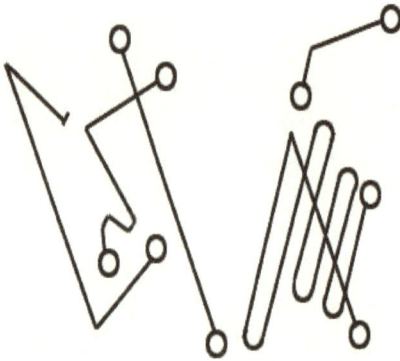

Sigil of Spirit:

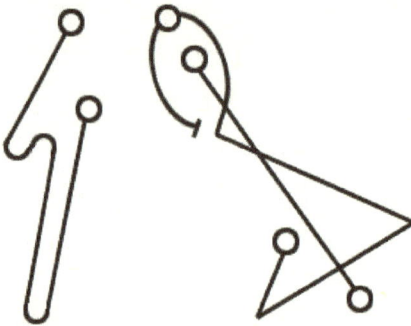

Sigil of Olympic Spirit:

Invocations of the Moon:

'O Levanah!
Thou who ruleth the secret kingdoms of ebb and flow, for
thee do I invoke this day by the mighty and potent name
SHADDAI EL CHAI,
The Almighty and Living God.
Hear me for thou art invoked in the name of thy holy
archangel Gabriel and by the might of the Kerubim.
Aid me with this my holy act of magic in the potent name
Shaddai el Chai!'

'Coniuro vos Levanah!
Coniuro in Domine SHADDAI EL CHAI!
Et in Domine archangelos Gabriel et per Kerebum sanctum!
Adiuvate nunc!'

Kameas: the Magical Squares

The planetary squares given above may seem irrelevant to your magic, but in fact they are a great aid for making talismans or other acts of planetary magic.

The square on each kamea will be the square of the planetary number, for example, the Moon has eighty-one small squares making up the kamea, eighty-one being 9 x 9, and nine being the number of the Moon. If, say, you were making a talisman of the Sun for yourself, a simple design would be to turn the letters of your name into numbers and then trace them on the solar kamea to give you the design for the talisman. This would be a good way not only to link with the energy concerned, but to personalise it.

Traditionally, our arte has used the Hebrew alphabet for this, as the letters of this alphabet all have numerical equivalents which allows the name of someone to be turned into numbers and then traced on the appropriate planetary kamea. However, I suggest that you use the schema from numerology.

Were we to make a talisman of the Sun for Joe Bloggs, who required it to help with his health problems, then we could do it this way.

Firstly, write out his name in numbers thus:

1	2	3	4	5	6	7	8	9
A	B	C	D	E	F	G	H	I
J	K	L	M	N	O	P	Q	R
S	T	U	V	W	X	Y	Z	

JOEBLOGGS

1 6 5 2 3 6 7 7 1

Then trace it on the Sun square, starting the line with a small circle at the beginning and a line at the end.

Joe Bloggs as a sigil on the solar kamea:

6	32	3	34	35	1
7	11	27	28	8	30
19	14	16	15	23	24
18	20	22	21	17	13
25	29	10	9	26	12
36	5	33	4	2	31

Now having started this work on a Sunday at the waxing Moon and having decided to make the talisman out of parchment instead of gold which, being the metal of the Sun, would work very well but would be expensive, we set to work thus:

Composing ourselves and considering the work and the outcome, so that we are clear in our head as to what we are working for; we start the work in the sure knowledge of success. Cut a circular piece of parchment say 2" in diameter and paint on to it some of the animating fluid that we made earlier, the fluid condenser. This, as you will recall, will hold like a battery the energies placed within the talisman. Using gold ink or paint, when our parchment has dried, draw on it a double circle like so and place the sigil of Joe Bloggs from the solar kamea in the middle. Around the edge and within the double circle write the god name that governs the solar current and the archangel's name also. Use the Theban script for this. On the back draw the seal of the planet.

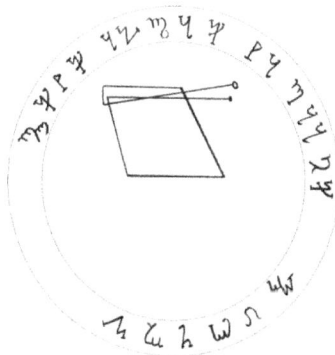

Joe Bloggs's name expressed as a sigil from the solar kamea

95

Working, if possible, within the solar hour of the day, set up your altar and workspace as you have done previously. Use gold or white candles on your altar and burn frankincense. A gold cloth on the altar would be appropriate, but if one is not available use white.

Let there be a nine-foot diameter circle if space allows, or smaller if need be, and draw an inner one six inches apart from the outer. Within this double circle write in the Theban script the God Name, the Archangel and the Order of Angels thus:

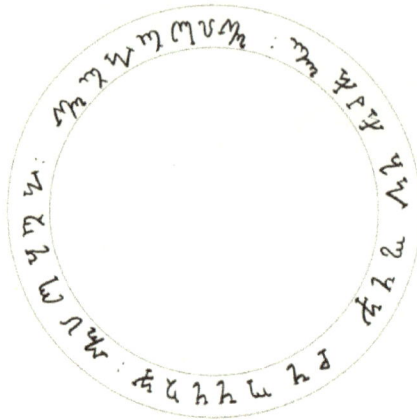

Now using the following formula, which must be adapted when working with other elemental or planetary energies, we proceed thus:

1: Clean physically your work space and place on your altar the altar cloth and candles, also athana, chalice, pentacle and wand. Facing east let the instruments of arte be in their elemental quarters upon the altar, that is, athana in the east, wand in the south, chalice in the west and the pentacle in the north.

2: Perform the Lesser Banishing Ritual of the Pentagram.

3: Sanctify the circle of arte with salt and water as previously shown.

4: The hallowing of the circle of arte with the elemental energies via the invoking pentagrams shown previously.

5: Declare the aims of the work.

6: Make a general oration to divinity, such as:

'Holy art thou lord of the Universe, Holy art thou whom nature hath not formed, Holy art thou God the vast and the mighty one, Thou who art lord of the   light and the darkness!'

Or some such of your own devising.

7: To declare your own divinity, use the *'Ol Sonuf Vaorsagi'* invocation.

8: Perform a further hallowing of your circle of arte with the invocation:

'I invoke thee, thou angels of the celestial spheres, thou whose dwelling is in the invisible etc'.

9: Rap on your altar the number of the planet, in this case, six knocks for the Sun. Using a solar invocation, trace the invoking solar hexagram over the altar.

10: Sprinkle the talisman with your holy water from the chalice declaring that all malignancy and hindrance is cast out forthwith and only the holy power of the planet that you are working with can enter herein, in this case the Sun. To further dedicate and consecrate the talisman, hold it in the rising incense smoke and declare your intent.

11: Having finished with the outer working, now proceed with the inner.

12: This can be done in a couple of ways such as building up around you the god image of the planet, in which case use the solar imagery of the crowned king. Another way would be to use the Middle Pillar working as already given.

However once you have established the pillar and circulations of light around your aura, you must then flood your aura with the solar current. Imagine that you are in a golden sphere, the brilliant and dazzling gold of the Sun and, as you do, chant either silently or audibly the God name of the Sun YHVH ALOAH VA DAATH and the archangel name Mikael. Feel yourself glowing with the power of the Sun, feel confident of success and know that it is real. Now see within your mind's eye that which you want to happen and know that it is true. Raising your right hand and holding the wand, which will be the outer symbol of your will, pour through it all the accumulated solar energy that you have aroused. Let it flow, via your wand, into the talisman, seeing it as a ball of the planetary colour involved. Look into this glowing ball, see your goal achieved and let the energy be absorbed by the talisman. Declaring *'As I do will, so mote it be!'*

13: Having done so, you must now take the talisman to the eastern quarter and hold it aloft, saying:

> *'O ye powers of Mizrach!*
> *Hear me!*
> *For this talisman is duly consecrated to achieve…*

(state again the intent).

> *As I do will so mote it be!'*

Perform the same in the south, west and north:

South: 'O ye powers of Darom!' etc,

West 'O ye powers of Mearab!' etc

North: 'O ye powers of Tzaphon!' etc

KNOW THAT IT IS TRUE!

14: Cover the talisman with silk as this is a psychic insulator and you don't want to banish the energies invoked during closing.

15: Trace the banishing solar hexagram over your altar whilst saying:

> *'I do give thanks to the mighty name YHVH ALOAH VA DAATH and to the holy archangel Mikael and unto the holy energies of Shemesh for assisting me, with this my holy act of magic.*
> *Let there be peace, grace and harmony between thee and me now and for always.*
> *For I too am a servant of the God most high!'*

16: Close with the following:

> *'Non nobis Domini non nobis'* etc.

17: Perform the Lesser Banishing Ritual of the Pentagram but using the relevant elemental pentagram at the appropriate quarter.

18: Knock ten times on the altar top to demonstrate your return to the everyday, ten being the number of Malkuth the everyday world that we live in. Do this as 3 + 3 + 3 + 1.

> *'Domini Unum Est'*

The completed talisman will better if wrapped in its own envelope and left to work without being bothered by you all the time. Carry it with you or place it somewhere where the individual that you are working on will pass by, or leave it undetected in their vicinity. The energies involved will do the work and do it well but like lightning they will take the short route to earth, so be mindful.

Another method of talisman construction, which is quicker and simpler, is to write down that which you want to occur. Think carefully about how you word this and then cross out any repeating letters. Then combine them into a sigil. All the letters that you use must be recognisable within the resultant figure.

JOE BLOGGS GOOD HEALTH

JOE BL~~O~~G~~GS~~ ~~GOO~~D HEA~~L~~T~~H~~

Thus leaving JOEBLGSDHAT

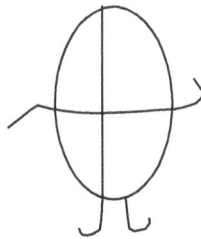

Placing the paper with the sigil on where you can see it clearly, you must hold your mind blank but concentrate on the sigil whilst you are brought to orgasm by self or with a partner. At the moment of release close your eyes momentarily.

Then let the sigil's image float down to the depths of your psyche, where it will gestate and the desire it symbolizes will by and by come to birth. Put the paper with the sigil somewhere safe and forget about the working. When the working has come about take the original sigil out and release it. This can be done by burning it solemnly.

Another potent aid to the success of your magical working is the use of the *psalms*. If you have read, or better still used, *Psalm* 109, the old cursing psalm, will know what I mean. I came across this many years ago in Thomas Hardy's novel *The Mayor of Casterbridge*; a most potent *psalm* indeed. Many people overlook the use of the *psalms* in their magic, which I think is a mistake, for they do have a lot of power, particularly when you think that they have been used for some two and a half thousand years. A lot of energy has been put into them and by the judicious use of them you can *'plug in'* to this power. It is there for the using regardless of your magical ethics (Ethics isn't that the county next door to Suffolk?).

If you look at the history of magic you will see that from the 17-19th centuries cunning men or women often used *psalms* in their magical work and very effectively too by all accounts. So there is a good magical tradition for this practice. *Psalms* can be used within and as part of a well-crafted piece of ritual or they can be used with something simpler like candle magic.

The following list of *psalms* have long been used for the aims stated and you may find them useful.

Psalms:

1: The protection of women and their children during pregnancy.

2: For protection from storms at sea.

3: Traditionally used for the healing of back and headaches.

4: Use three times before sunrise to reverse runs of bad luck.

5: To gain favour from those in authority. Pray this psalm over some olive oil at both sunrise and sunset then anoint thy head.

6: Good for health concerns

7: If persecuted by slanders and by those who would do you ill, then use this psalm and throw a handful of dust in their general direction.

8: This psalm is useful to gain the favours of others that will promote your business.

9: Useful to turn the tide against thine enemies and to the promotion of good health in young male children.

10: This is a good psalm to quieten a disturbed spirit.

11/12/13: Will protect from evil.

14: Will promote goodwill from your neighbours.

15: Good to quieten troubled souls:

16: Can be used to turn enemies into friends and to promote good luck and the return of stolen things.

17: Use for healing and for protection.

18: Use to promote good health.

19: Used in exorcism and the dispelling of bad vibes.

20: Traditionally used to gain the favour of a judge.

21: To gain favour from those in position of power.

22: Will protect the utterer on journeys from all peril.

23: Useful in gaining answers in dreams to your troubles.

24/25/26: Used in rites of protection.

27: To gain favour from those who can help you.

28: To gain the friendship of your enemy use this psalm.

30: Traditionally used to dispel bad vibes.

31: Very good to protect from slander.

32: Promotes good luck and well-being.

33: Protects children.

34: Good for the promotion of a safe journey and for the gaining of favours from those in authority.

35: Used to gain justice in a court case.

36: Protects against libel and slander.

37: Used to clear hangovers (useful)

38/39: To be believed in court use both of these psalms.

40: Good to promote peace in a disturbed environment.

41/43: Traditionally used to regain what you have lost through the actions of another

42: To gain answers in your dreams.

44: To be safe from your enemies.

45/46: Promotes peace within a relationship.

47: Good to gain favours.

48: To stop the persecution of you by your enemies.

49/50: Useful to promote the health of members of your family.

51: To gain forgiveness and peace of mind for thine sins.

52: Use to stop the bad actions of those who are against you.

53/55: Good for the protection against the actions of your enemies.

54: To gain revenge on thine enemies.

56: To resist temptation.

57: For good luck.

58: Protection against dangerous animals.

59: Protection from doing the wrong thing.

60: To gain victory over your adversary.

61: Good for blessing a new house.

62: Promotes contact with divinity.

63: Use to gain advantage over business rivals.

64: Promotes a safe journey at sea.

65: Used to gain favour.

66: Traditionally used in some quarters in exorcism.

67/68: Useful in exorcism: recite over a bowl of clean water and then asperge the area.

69/70: Recite over clean water and wash therein; this will help to break bad habits.

71: Good for the release from difficult situations.

72: Brings good luck and favours.

73: Protection.

74: Brings retribution and frustration to one's enemies.

75: Brings peace of mind.

76: Provides protections from perils.

77: Grants relief from want.

78: The use of this psalm grants favours from those above you.

79: Fatal to enemies and those who oppose you.

80/81: Promotes sound judgment.

82: Good for business.

83: Provides protection.

84: By washing in the waters over which this psalm has been said, the relieving of all manner of ills may be acquired.

85: Promotes friendship.

86-88: Useful in providing goodwill.

89: This psalm will be found to be of use in the promoting of good health.

90/91: Will be extremely useful to assist with protection from all dangers.

92: Good to gain favour.

93: The reciting of this psalm will assist in the winning of lawsuits.

94: This psalm will gain you the advantage over an opponent.

95: Helps to promote understanding.

96/97: Useful to gain good luck.

98: Promotes peace.

99: Use this psalm to gain peace of mind.

100/101: Used to overcome one's enemies.

102/103: Traditionally used to overcome barrenness.

104: Overcomes evil.

105-107: These three psalms will promote good health.

108: Good for success in business.

109: Will definitely promote bad luck upon your enemies.

110-113: Good to overcome your enemies.

114: Will promote business success.

115: With the power of this psalm you will gain the best of arguments and debates.

116: Regular use of this psalm will protect those who utter it from dangers.

117: Helps to cope with bad actions.

118: Confounds those who would oppose you.

119: Used in the healing of all ills.

120: Good to win in a court case.

121: This psalm will provide protection whilst travelling at night.

122: Will grant favours from those in positions above you.

123: Good to return lost or stolen property.

124: Will promote safe travel by water.

125: Traditionally used to overcome enemies.

126: Has always been regarded as having the power to bring people to you.

127: Provides protection.

128: Provides safety in pregnancy.

129: Good to promote good deeds.

130: Considered potent in the providing of safety.

131: Stops one from making bad judgments.

132: Will help to break bad habits.

133: Good for the promotion of friendships.

134: This psalm will help you to be studious.

135: Traditionally used to promote stronger links with divinity.

137: Overcomes hate and malice.

138-139: Good for the gaining of love and friendship.

140: Restores peace.

141: Removes fear.

142-144: These three psalms will help to promote good health.

145: Good to provide peace in a disturbed atmosphere.

146-147: These two psalms will promote good health and the overcoming of ill health.

148-150: Provides protection from danger.

Candle Magic:

The use of consecrated and charged candles to work a piece of magic is something well-known, indeed the Catholics have been doing it for centuries. You can charge a candle of the appropriate planetary colour and light it. The energies will then be released to do your will. Always try and burn a little of the incense of the planet or element concerned. You could, if you so wished, work your candle magic within a full planetary ritual, but it need not be so. However, clear your work area with the Lesser Banishing Ritual of the Pentagram, an invocation to divinity would not be out of place, and one to the planetary energies that you are working with. Take some consecrated water and bless, dedicate and make holy your candle of the arte.

Holding it in the rising incense smoke, declare your intent, take the candle, and rub oil from the middle of it to the wick and then from the middle to the base whilst concentrating on the goal of your desire. The oil could be of the planetary nature suitable for the work or, if not available, olive oil. You could at this point also use the Middle Pillar exercise as previously shown. After strongly visualising your intent, pour the energies into the candle and then light it. Place the candle where it is safe, so that it will not fall over and burn your house down. This is very important! You could use the candle over several workings if you don't want to leave it unattended. For example, when you have charged the candle with whatever method that you decide, you could burn it at the same time every day for several days or until it is consumed, whilst staring into its flame and seeing your will being accomplished.

Although I would say that you should use a candle of the appropriate colour for this work this is, in my experience, not strictly necessary. I have used white candles for all sorts of candle magic just by visualising it in its planetary colour. This I know works, whether you be working for good or ill. This colour schema, I know, goes against modern teachings on candle magic but consider how things were in the Middle Ages: the most common candles would have been whitish depending on how fine the beeswax or the tallow had been refined. The use of coloured candles is a boon of the times that we live in and not a strict necessity.

How long does it take for the magic to work? I would expect it to work within a lunar month unless you are working on a bigger time scale for a long-term effect.

Fixed Stars in Magic:

The power of the stars was something that was used extensively in medieval magic. Certain stars were considered to be favourable for a variety of purposes. Their energies were, and indeed are, accessed by the use of the relevant imagery and incense. They may be made into useful talismans and can be constructed and consecrated using the methods of our arte. They can also be carved upon a candle and invoked via candle magic. The following fifteen stars and their symbols will be found to be of use to the sorcerer/ess.

1: Aldebaran: Gives riches and honour. Image: a flying man. Incense: milk thistle.

2: Algol: Grants success and favours. Turns back bad actions on the doer thereof. Image: A human head. Incense: mugwort.

3: Algorab: Makes the wearer courageous. It gives protection from malice. It has the power to summon or drive away evil spirits. Image: a raven. Incense: comfrey.

4: Alphecca: Promotes the goodwill of men. Image: a hen or a crowned man. Incense: rosemary.

5: Antares: Banishes evil spirits. Image: a man in armour. Incense: saffron.

6: Arcturus: Cures fevers. Image: either a dancing man or a horse or a wolf. Incense: plantain.

7: Capella: Makes the wearer honoured above others. Image: a man playing a musical instrument. Incense: mandrake or mugwort.

8: Pleiades: Good to find out secrets, raises winds and improves eyesight. Image: a young girl or a lamp. Incense: fennel or frankincense.

9: Polaris: Gives safety when travelling and protects the wearer from evil. Image: a bull or a calf. Incense: periwinkle.

10: Procyon: Preserves health, grants the favours of all and protects against witchcrafts of all sorts. Image: Three small girls or a cockerel. Incense: marigold flowers or pennyroyal.

11: Regulus: Grants favours. Image: a cat or a lion. Incense: mastic.

12: Sirius: Gives honour, promotes peace and goodwill. Image: a dog. Incense: mugwort.

13: Vega: Gives power over animals and devils. Makes the wearer noble of spirit. Image: a vulture or a hen. Incense: fumitory.

The Magical Seals of the Fixed Stars:

Aldebaran:

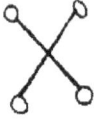

Pleiades:

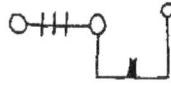

Algol:

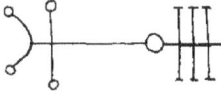

Polaris:

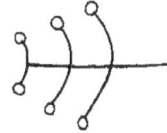

Algorab:

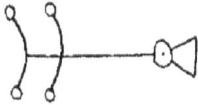

Procyon:

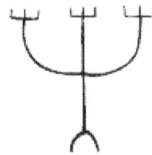

Alphecca:

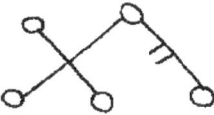

Regulus:

Antares:

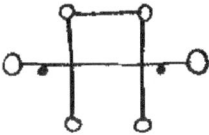

Sirius:

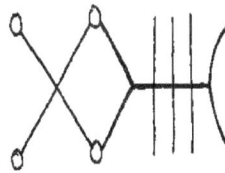

Arcturus:

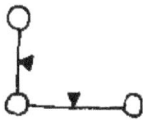

Vega:

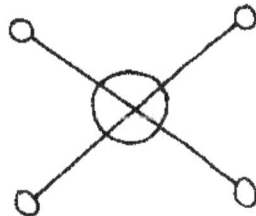

Capella:

Poppets:

These have a well-known association with magic. The making of a doll to influence someone for good or ill is an old practice. What you are doing with your magic is enacting out that which you want to happen, with the intent that it will. Poppets can be used within a binding ritual or one of cursing, they can be used to promote love and desire between people, or used to help the healing process - they are extremely useful.

To make one you will need to fashion out of wax or clay a figure to represent the person intended, they can also be manufactured out of plasticene or made from cloth as a rag doll. However, they will all need something of a personal nature from the individual to identify the doll with the person concerned. They will also be more potent and alive if you add some of your animating fluid, the fluid condenser that we concocted in chapter four.

Whether your ritual be one of healing, love, or destruction or binding, you will need to work the planetary rites that are relevant to your work. Then, in the ritual, the poppet must be consecrated and named to be the person concerned. Baptise it with your consecrated water of the arte. Hold it in the incense smoke and know that it is the person so named. Now lay it on your altar top and see the poppet live and breathe, know that this is so and that which now happens to the poppet happens to that person. See the poppet as that person. If you were invoking love between two people, then you will have made two poppets, one for each person concerned. Use the Middle Pillar working in your rite to connect with the, in this case Venusian, energies and pour the charged light into the poppets. See that which you have willed, coming to pass and bind them tight with a green cord face to face. Now the future has no escape. Wrap them in a cloth of the appropriate colour and after the rite put them away safely and out of sight. Do not disturb!

Ritual such as this will need to be worked in the right planetary hour and day; also in the right lunar phase.

Another method of magical working is to use the seals of the *Goetia* demons from the *Lesser Key of Solomon*. Whilst this is a specialist system of magic and you will need to have a good measure of proficiency for this type of work, it can, in my experience, work very quickly. I once had recourse to work with one of these entities to solve a problem and as soon as the ritual had finished and everything had been put away, out of the blue someone rang with the answer to the problem. They can work quickly when needed to. An account of working with these energies is given in the excellent book by Lon DuQuette, *My Life with the Spirits*, a book that I highly recommend. We will look at this type of working in more detail in chapter eight.

CHAPTER SIX

Finding things out

'Heaven's imprint on earth'

As a sorcerer/ess there will be times when you want to find things out and find them out quickly. One of the problems of divination is that you can be led astray by your own wants and needs and consequently get an inaccurate reading. Two systems of divination that have stood the test of time, because they work and can get around this problem, are horary astrology and geomancy.

Geomancy is a system that can give quick yes or no answers; it can also go into greater depth with an answer. Because of its simplicity and accuracy I am surprised that it is not more widely known. It is based on sixteen symbols which traditionally have been generated from making dots in a tray of sand at random; although you can do the same with a pen on a piece of paper.

But we will, in the best traditions of our arte, make and use rune sticks, as these are unequivocal in their answers. Early on a Wednesday morning, when the Moon is waxing, take yourself off to a hazel tree that you have already approached and explained your need to. Now, if it feels right, cut a stick with your knife of arte, say half an inch thick, a stick that can be cut into four equal lengths of nine inches. When you are back home peel it and shave it flat on both sides. In the middle of each stick paint with black paint one dot on one side and two dots on the other side, again in the middle. When they are dry, bless and dedicate them to the accuracy of your readings with them by using the familiar skills of our arte. When not in use, keep them wrapped in clean cloth, silk would be ideal.

They are used thus.

Contemplate your question and take the four sticks from their covering cloth. Lay this out on the floor before you. This is now your work surface. Stand them upright one at a time and between both hands, spin the rune stick between your palms and let it drop on to the cloth. If there is one dot upright then place one dot on a sheet of paper if two dots then place two dots on the paper. Take the other sticks one at a time and repeat, place the dot(s) in order underneath the one cast previously. You will have now created a symbol composed of four lines of either one or two dots to the line. Repeat this operation another three times so that you have four symbols before you thus. Naturally it will be unlikely that you will have the following symbols in the following order but I give these as a demonstration.

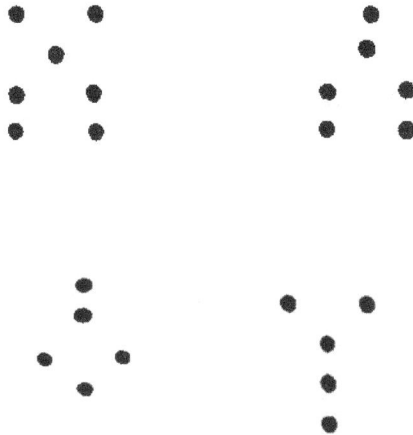

These four figures are known as the mothers and from them are generated eight new figures, plus the two witnesses and the judge. The judge will give a yes or no answer.

To create these, starting with the first figure, take the dots from the first line; these make the first line of the fifth figure. The first line of the second figure makes the second line of the fifth figure, whilst the first line of the third makes the third line and the first line of the fourth figure the fourth and last line of the fifth figure. Using this formula three more times, the second lines of the mothers make the sixth figure and the third and fourth lines of the mothers make the seventh and eight figures respectively.

These new figures are the daughters. In our example, the following are generated from the mothers above.

Now the last four figures are generated thus. Add together the first lines from figures one and two; this will make the first line of figure nine. Do the same with the second lines from the first and second figures. These will make the second line of the ninth figure. The third and the fourth lines from figures one and two will make the third and the fourth lines of figure nine respectively. Do the same with figures three and four to produce figure ten and repeat the same process with the fifth and sixth figures to make figure eleven and use the figures seven and eight to produce figure number twelve, as seen below.

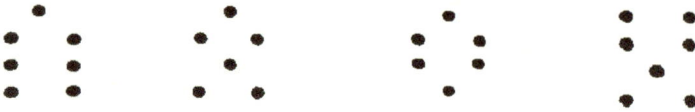

Add the figures nine and ten together as previously shown, thus using the rules of our arte to produce the first witness. Place this on the right; this will refer to past events regarding your question. Then, by adding together in a likewise manner figures eleven and twelve, produce the second witness, and place this on the left. This figure will comment on the future.

By adding together both witnesses we will produce the judge, which will give a yes or no answer. If it is a good figure then the answer is yes, if it is a bad figure then the answer will be a no. A negative judge that is produced from two bad figures is a definite no and you are strongly advised that it is in your interest to accept this. If it is made from one good and one bad figure, then the matter enquired about, will go from good to bad. A negative judgment that is made from two good figures still means no, but it won't be too bad a result. With a good judge made from two good figures, then it is to be considered a definite yes. If a good figure is made from two bad figures, it is still a yes answer, but there will be problems. A judge made from one good and one bad figure will be a yes answer but the outcome will not be that good.

These are the final three figures in our example.

2nd witness refers to the future, 1st witness refers to the past

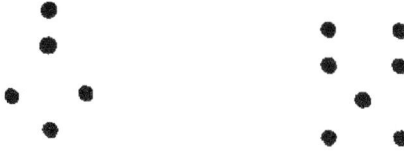

Judge giving yes or no answers

The figure of the judge is Carcer which is a definite no answer to the question. The right figure (the 1st witness referring to the past) is Albus which is a good figure because it is associated with peace. The left figure (the 2nd witness referring to the future) Puella is also a good figure. Thus in our example we have a no answer from two good figures, which despite the positive indications is still answering negatively.

The Sixteen Geomantic Figures:

PUER (Boy) Unfavourable figure except for love or war. Its planet is Mars. This figure is one of rashness, violence and destruction. Good in the third and sixth houses but bad in the fifth.

AMISSIO (Loss) Often represents something that's just outside one's reach. Generally a figure of loss. Bad for gain but good for love. Its planet is Venus.

ALBUS (White) A weak figure but favourable. Good for beginnings and profit. Its planet is Mercury.

POPULA (People) Good with a good figure and bad with bad figures. This is a neutral figure and its planet is the Moon.

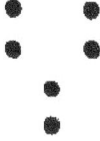

FORTUNA MAJOR (Greater Fortune)   This figure confirms a positive outcome and is favourable in any situation. Its planet is the Sun.

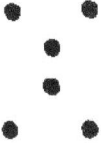

CONJUNCTIO (Conjunction) A neutral figure that promotes good with good or bad with bad. Mercury is its planet.

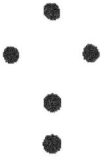

PUELLA (Girl)   A favourable figure good for happiness and harmony but can be fickle. Its planet is Venus.

RUBEUS (Red) An unfavourable figure one of violence and vice. Evil in good and good in evil. Its planet is Mars.

```
  •   •
    •
  •   •
    •
```

ACQUISITIO (Gain) Good for all material matters. This is a positive figure, a figure of success and good fortune. Its planet is Jupiter.

```
    •
  •   •
  •   •
    •
```

CARCER (Prison) Although this is an unfavourable figure, being one of binding and restrictions, it is good for stability and buildings. Its planet is Saturn. Good in the fourth and twelfth house but unfavourable in the sixth, seventh and eighth.

```
  •   •
  •   •
  •   •
    •
```

TRISTITIA (Sorrow) An unfavourable figure except for questions regarding the earth or buildings. Bad in all houses except for the fourth, eight and twelfth. Its planet is Saturn.

```
    •
  •   •
  •   •
  •   •
```

LAETITIA (Joy) Favourable in all questions. Good in the fifth and eleventh houses but not so in the sixth, eight and twelfth. Its planet is Jupiter.

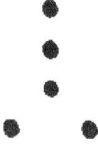

CAUDA DRACONIS (Dragon's Tail) Generally an unfavourable figure. This is a figure of loss and it does not bode well when in the second, fourth or eleventh houses. Its planet is the southern node of the Moon, the 'Dragons Tail'.

CAPUT DRACONIS (Head of the Dragon) This is a good figure and is one of favourable beginnings and profit. It is good in the second, fifth, seventh and eleventh. Not good in the twelfth house. Its planet is the north node of the Moon, the 'Dragon's Head'.

FORTUNA MINOR (Lesser Fortune) This is a symbol of good fortune but it is also a figure of change and instability. Favourable in the second, eighth and ninth houses. Its planet is the Sun.

VIA (The Way) This figure is unfavourable in all things except travel. It is a symbol of change and an alternation between good and bad fortune. Favourable in the third, fifth and seventh houses. Not good in the eleventh house.

A geomantic chart can be laid out to give an in-depth answer to a query thus. This chart is set in the manner of a medieval horoscope, it may very well seem unintelligible but it does have its own logic, which works. Following a house interpretation from astrology the houses are thus:

1st: Deals with the individual, it will describe them in some way. This house will represent the querent, ie the person for whom the reading is being done.

2nd: Money and lost possessions. Or as tradition says *'One's moveable goods.'*

3rd: News of any event, short journeys, brothers and sisters.

4th: The end of any matter, the home and your father.

5th: Sex, children, speculation and entertainment. Your father's finances.

6th: Health, work, your uncles and aunts. Servants and animals smaller than a goat.

7th: Partner, wife, friends and your known enemies.

8th: Partner's finances, wills and legacies, occult matters, taxes and social security benefits. Death.

9th: Long journeys, education, banks, church matters, partner's brothers and sisters

10th: Mother, one's career and public standing,

11th: Mother's finances, partner's children, hopes and wishes.

12th: Hospitals, prisons, secret enemies and events, animals larger than a goat, witchcraft matters, also being confined in some manner.

Look to the house relevant to what your question is about. If it is of a financial matter then consider the second house. Is there a good or bad figure therein? Is it supported by good or bad figures either side? What figure opposes it? (This would be the house number eighth in this matter) Is this a good or bad figure? If it is bad, then how bad, this would be where you can expect opposition from. Also, consider the figures that are square to the house in question. In astrology squares are ninety degrees apart, in geomantic charts they will be the houses that are at right angles to the one of the question. Therefore the fifth and the eleventh houses will be square to the second house. Square houses will show where you can expect problems from; however if a good figure is deposited in one of these then there will be no problems from that quarter - if a bad figure then read accordingly.

The houses that are trine are also to be considered. Trines in astrology are the aspects that are one hundred and twenty degrees apart. Or in this case they will be the houses that are a third of the way around the chart from the one enquired about. Therefore the sixth and the tenth houses are the ones that are trined to the second. These houses will show any support that can be expected. Bad figures here show no support, good figures on the other hand show support and what kind and where from.

Also consider sextiles, which are sixty degrees apart in astrology but in geomancy the houses halfway between the house of the question and the trines - in this case the fourth and the twelfth houses. Sextiles are good but not as good as trines, they will show helpful influences if any. Bad figures here will show no helpful influences.

If Rubeus falls in the first house, then unless it is a question of magic or war then destroy the figure and start again later, as this is not the time to answer the question proposed.

SOUTH

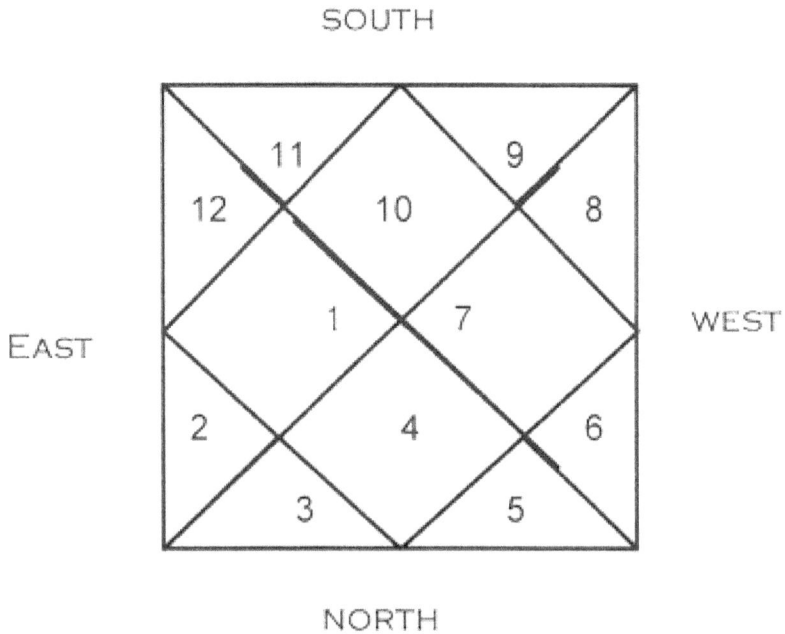

EAST

WEST

NORTH

Placement of geomantic figures within the houses:

1st figure place in the 10th house

2nd figure place in the 1st house

3rd figure place in the 4th house

4th figure place in the 7th house

5th figure place in the 11th house

6th figure place in the 2nd house

7th figure place in the 5rd house

8th figure place in the 8th house

9th figure place in the 12th house

10th figure place in the 3rd house

11th figure place in the 6th house

12th figure place in the 9th house

CHAPTER SEVEN

'If I turn the other cheek will you hit that too?'

Human nature being what it is, we inevitably fall foul of someone or another at some time in our lives. With egos that get hurt, or pride which becomes dented, we then seethe with indignation. But it's no bad thing to have one's ego or pride placed in check from time to time. Self-pride is no bad thing, providing that you are not completely overtaken with it and a little, compared to a lot, is to be encouraged, as we all need to feel good about ourselves to get the best from ourselves.

But that doesn't mean that we should get too big for our boots unless, of course, we can afford a bigger pair of boots. However tempting it becomes to strike back at someone when we feel that they have deserved it, is it wise to do so?

By that, I am not suggesting that you should be too bogged down with modern wishy-washy notions of karma and the wiccan so-called *'law of threefold return,'* that is, whatever it is that you do will return threefold back to you. Myself, I don't believe it, as I think it was invented by the founders of the modern wiccan/witchcraft revival to encourage society to think that they, modern witches/wiccans, were nice people and those modern witches, or those who think they are, are a little misunderstood by society, but kindly folk just the same.

After all, if you are to be condemned because you bind someone, or curse them, how much more the arms dealer, the dodgy politician, the crooked banker and other unsavoury folk that can and do bring untold misery to millions of people on the earth? As for the victim of your binding or cursing, it could have been part of that individual's fate that they should carry on in some manner until they cross somebody who is angered enough to work against them.

For example, I know someone who stopped somebody who had a habit of shooting at cats with a catapult and pointed out that it was better if they saw the error of their ways and stopped doing it. Not that the request was taken any notice of. So, on the dark of the Moon, they performed a cursing ritual to bring them down like the cats. This was done with the earth element in its negative binding and blocking aspects. They based it on the use of the earth fluid condensers and sigils from chapter four. So at night, armed with the fully charged talisman, they buried it in the garden of the victim, with the intent that as it rotted the magic would come to birth. It did, some weeks later: the individual had a stroke and became partly paralysed and thereafter left the cats alone, although I don't know what happened to the catapult. Was this the magic or was it the workings of fate? Would the individual have gone on and had a stroke anyway? Or did the magic tip the balance? If they had come around the corner five minutes later they may very well not have found out about the shooting of the cats. So therefore, was the individual concerned destined to be cursed? Although I would say that if they had left the cats alone then the individual concerned would not have been cursed. So these things are not black or white as some folk seem to think they are. But whatever you do, think hard about it.

My great-grandmother Emma King, who was a cunning woman from the fen country, once said that if you lay a curse and miss your target that it is then that it will return to you. So all I can say is that your aim had better be good. These days, owing to occult political correctness, there is very little information about regarding the binding and cursing of someone or something, but there are several traditional spells and works that owing to their age are extremely potent and very useful.

The following work, which will promote bad feelings, to say the least, between two people, is, I am reliably informed, a traditional spell from the fourteenth century. All I can say is it works!

At the wane of the Moon, hunt out two stones from a brook or a river. Take the stones home and back to your workspace. Carve, or mark on the one stone the name of the one person and on the other, the name of the second person. On stone number one also carve the following: Cartutay, Momabel, Sobil and Geteritacon. On stone number two inscribe the following names: Puzanil, Pimaton, Folfitoy and Mansator.

These names are considered highly antipathetic to one another. Ideally, bury the one stone somewhere over which person number one will walk and stone number two somewhere the second person will walk. Otherwise, if not practicable, then bury them at a crossroads or in a graveyard. Let the stones remain there for seven days and nights.

The following morning, early if possible, better still at sunrise, remove the stones and take them home where you must throw them on to a fire saying:

'I conjure thee O most inimical spirits, by the glory of the everlasting God to sow and arouse much hatred between X and Y, whose names are carved here on these stones.'

Now lift the stones from the fire saying:

'When their fury is enkindled against them, perhaps the waters will swallow them up.' (from Psalm 123).

Take the stones and cast them into cold water, where you must leave them for three days and nights. On the fourth day remove them from the waters and cense them with a martial incense, like opoponax or dragon's blood.

Saying:

*'I conjure thee, thou hateful and malignant, invidious and discordant demons
to arouse a great hatred between X and Y.
Arouse and inflame them
so that they cannot stand the sight of one another.
Inflict them with an immeasurable hatred for each other.
Let all affection and friendship be thus removed and let there be enmity and utter hatred between them.'*

Let this be said thrice with constant suffumigations with the martial incense. Place the two stones in the dark and the next night, take the two stones from their hiding place and strike hard together (mind your fingers) saying:

*'I do not smash these stones, but I smash X and Y together,
whose names are written here,
so that they will inflict
the utmost hatred upon each other.'*

Repeat this for three nights and the magic will be brought to birth.

To further estrange the victims you can, if you so will, wait until the Sunday before the new Moon, better still if it is at the very dark of the Moon, then just before sunrise, take the stones out into the open and walk towards the sunrise.

Then you must bang the stones together, saying as you did before, *'I do not smash these stones but X and Y'* etc. Now bury the one and walk in the opposite direction from the buried stone. Draw a furrow in the soil so that it becomes a dividing line between the two stones and walk on until you are the same distance or thereabouts from the furrow that the first buried stone is. Here bury the second stone and say:

> 'As I have separated these stones,
> thus is X and Y separated never to be united.
> Let them be as distant as these stones.'

See them quarrelling and being apart from one another. Keep this working secret, for in silence was it conceived and let silence attend its birth.

Owing to the power of suggestion, curses and ill wishing can become a self-fulfilling prophecy and all you have to do is give it a nudge in the right direction. For example a sorcerer of my acquaintance took umbrage at a New Age Cosmic shop that had moved into his locality, considering that they definitely lowered the tone of the occult with their tacky rubbish, of which he said *I would not give dustbin space to'*. Ouch! However it was apparently obvious, or so I was told, that despite trying to be the local leaders on the occult scene these chumps hadn't got a clue. This was demonstrated by the fact that, although he did nothing apart from asking some searching questions, they became convinced that he had cursed the shop and that his very presence brought fear to the staff and the owner thereof, whenever he walked past (which wasn't very often). They blamed him for their lack of customers and everything that went wrong, so much so that they moved town and lost several thousands of pounds in the process. Yet the fools had actually cursed themselves and his occasional presence just reinforced it.

Such can be the power of suggestion. You could ask where was their magic? If you can convey the idea to your victim that they have been ill wished or cursed, even non-believers who scoff have been known to change their minds, albeit reluctantly. It is surprising how anything that goes wrong can then be attributed to your actions, so much so that it can have a snowballing effect. If you have a taste for the theatrical then physical confrontation can work wonders.

Many years ago an old witch I knew, who had for no apparent reason (well not one that I knew of) had been banned from a pub nearby where she lived. One day she burst into the full bar and standing only on her left foot, and pointing her fully stretched left arm at the owner, the fist being clenched with the first two fingers pointing, she glanced along it with her left eye, the right one being closed and she delivered her curse. With the swirls of the heavy black cloak that she perpetually wore and the clack of the elephant hide clogs on her feet, at five foot nothing and in a rage, she could command a presence. The publican was told in no uncertain manner that he would be gone in x amounts of weeks. Strangely enough, the man sold up and left town not long after this incident and in the time scale stated. If you do go down the road of physical confrontation it may be no bad thing, particularly, in the early stages of your career, to go back home and reinforce the work with a magical working that is appropriate to the curse.

By now, I would expect you to realise that you use Saturnine energies for bindings and martial forces for destruction.

One traditional magical working is ligature: the magical binding to prevent a certain action. This is a saturnine operation and can be performed thus.

On a waning Moon, better on a Saturday and if possible in the hour of Saturn, set up the circle of arte, invoking the energies of Saturn. You will need to acquire a black cord and something of a personal nature relating to the other person that is being bound, such as an article of unwashed clothing or some strands of hair.

As part of your saturnine invocations, dwell on the imagery of Saturn and see with your visualising skills before and about you, a tall dark woman: she walks between two pillars accompanied by an owl. It is winter and night has fallen, the air is cold and the landscape is barren. She leans heavily on an old blackthorn staff and she carries a burning torch, which smokes heavily. In the distance is a crescent waning Moon, which hangs low in the night sky and shines with a pale glimmer. Let this imagery create shivers within you.

Then take up the cord. Dip this in the chalice and dedicate it to the success of your operation and now cense it in the rising incense smoke, which should, of course, be myrrh. Anoint the cord with a drop of civet oil and see the cord spark. Let the oil be the mark of the fire of your desire, the energy of your undaunted will. As you bind the hair or clothing with the cord, see that the person being bound is unable to perform the actions that you are working against. As you visualise this intone firmly and deliberately the following words of intent:

> 'Hear me X, for I conjure thee that by night your eyes are blinded and by clay your ears are stopped. For by earth your mouth is sealed and by rock your limbs are bound

Now hear these words addressed to thee FOR THIS MY WILL,
SO MOTE IT BE!'

Take the cord somewhere secret and safe, a churchyard perhaps, or a silent part of your garden. Here dig a little hole and bury the cord and place a stone on top of the grave and as you do this, say:

'Twist and tangled art thou, O, X
and never shalt thee rise up again.
For your eyes are dimmed and your limbs are bound as thou
art laid in the deep and silence of the ground.'

To release them from your wrath, you must, on a waxing Moon, dig up the cords with the declared intent that you are freeing them from the bondage that you have imposed upon them. You must see it as so and untie them.

This binding work could also be done with a poppet to good effect. The poppet could be placed in a box and sealed, or covered in a black cloth and placed somewhere dark, or even buried. All would work well. Someone I once knew used to place a sigil of the individual's name (I would presume that the sigil would be taken from the Mars Square), in an iron box, wire it tight and during the ritual roast it over an open fire, with suitable invocations appertaining to the work; this, I was assured, worked to great effect. So, there is plenty of scope to be individualistic in your workings.

Indeed, my acquaintance, the sorcerer mentioned earlier, once told me how he performed a cursing solely with a scourge and some martial incense. Having had enough of a local bully making his children's lives a misery, he in a fury entered his temple and enkindled some dragon's blood, during which he built up the imagery before him of the individual concerned and in his wrath he thrashed the image with his scourge, declaring that the person was well and truly cursed. He wielded the scourge so hard that he told me that it broke in the air. As I knew he had made it himself, I did wonder if it was poorly made and that had something to do with it, but I didn't dare ask. Anyway, within weeks the bully was picked up for drunk driving and lost his licence, next he lost his job, then he lost his girlfriend after which he started to lose his friends, perhaps they thought he was bad luck. More importantly he stopped being a bully. Once again, this is a working like the catapulting of the cats that happened because an individual would not stop their nasty ways. Neither works were done for spite nor for the sake of doing them out of curiosity; they were felt however, to be relevant to the actions of the moment.

Another working that is simple to perform is the following: take some salt and coriander, and mix with some dragon's blood. This can all, though it need not be, performed in our circle of arte. However, do this working on the waning Moon preferably on a Tuesday, Mars' day. In the dark and silence of the night light the charcoal in your censer and make it glow red and hot, then in the glimmering candle light visualise the transgressor who trespasses against your will. Keeping the cursing short (better still if you can pronounce it in rhyming couplets), throw some of the mixture onto the glowing charcoal and watch it burn. See in the rising incense smoke the realisation of your will and know that it is coming to pass. Repeat this operation three times with as much intent and burning desire that your energies can muster. This is a simple but effective work that can bring results quickly. Of course you could make a talisman, using our arte as suggested earlier, to bring such effects into being, or even candle magic. The choice is yours.

One final working that uses the whole might of our arte is the use of the poppet within a well-crafted ritual. In this case wait until the waning of the Moon and on a Tuesday, in the hour of Mars, cast the circle of arte and invoke the powers of the red planet.

Taking the poppet, that has been made according to our rules, inscribe on the back the name of the person and underneath the old names of power: Cabye, Aaaze, Hit, Fel, Meltat. Let the poppet be baptised with the consecrated waters of arte and held in the burning suffumigations from the censer. See it as the person named. Watch it breathe and live. Taking a thorn from the blackthorn tree that you collected earlier, a thorn again dedicated to the outcome of your will, thrust it in the doll at the point where you will and see the infliction happening as it comes to birth.

Whilst this working can be repeated more than once, I will point out that owing to the energies involved, you may find this operation a little draining. It can, if done with force enough, feel as if you have been wrung out to dry. However it soon passes. You must cover the poppet with a silken cloth or at least a black cloth. Be forceful in the closure and winding down of this ritual, as the energies involved will have to be firmly banished to whence they came. Put the poppet somewhere safe, in the dark and out of sight. You could bury it but if you do, remember where it is, so that you can retrieve it, if you so wish, at a later stage.

Do not start these types of operations if you are lukewarm about the outcome. It is no good once you have started to feel that perhaps you shouldn't be doing this. You must be certain in your intent and beyond compassion for those who have invoked your wrath. Be absolutely clear, this type of working must be entered into wholeheartily and not with reservations. This is primarily because if you do not then the working is unlikely to succeed and more importantly you are laying yourself open for the current, however lightly invoked, to miss the target and to then manifest in your own life.

If not using a martial incense, then use one that has traditionally been used for wrath and chastisement, such as this one: in the hour of Mars and at the waning of the Moon, take equal amounts of dragon's blood, rue and such herbs as the following, but in half the amounts that you took for the dragon's blood: peppercorns, ginger, dry nettles and blackthorn leaves (sometimes called strafe). Blend these together and put away safely until needed.

Protection:

Once you have learnt to go on the attack it is no bad thing to know how to defend yourself. I am not suggesting that you must be on a twenty-four hour standby, with a flaming sword to see off those who are planning to get you, but there are everyday little things that are useful to know as one wends one's way through life. It will be uncommon to experience a full-scale occult assault, despite the fact that some folk think that there are always, seemingly, nasties that have been sent to get them and to make their (not the nasties') life uncomfortable. I wonder if the nasties ever think *'What have I done, to have to haunt this idiot?'* Sometimes auras can be punctured and they can leak energy, then the person will feel lethargic and run down.

I have known this to happen to someone who had taken a Reiki healing from a dubious individual. For a couple of weeks they were feeling ill, complaining of stomach pains and cramps. When they told me about it, I suspected that the Reiki healer had done something. Not knowing about Reiki I read up on the subject and soon realised that their solar plexus was leaking their life force. With this, I promptly suggested that they performed the Lesser Banishing Ritual of the Pentagram and burned some frankincense. Then, taking some consecrated water, they traced a banishing pentagram over the solar plexus, with the firm intent that they were closing the leakage and that the link between themselves and the dubious Reiki healer was broken. Afterwards they then went through the Middle Pillar exercise and flooded their aura with the brilliance of their divinity. Within ten minutes of this working they were feeling much better and all the stomach problems that they were having ceased, they quickly had all their old energy levels restored. So much for Reiki! Whilst you are perhaps unlikely to experience this sort of attack, the everyday will throw up a host of tensions and difficult situations for you.

For example, next time you are in a conversation with someone, be it simple and light-hearted, or one where you need to be assertive, try holding their gaze by staring at the spot between their eyebrows. This will soon throw them and they will avert their eyes, and then come back to stare at you. All you have to do is repeat the gesture which will cause them then to try harder to stare at you. The thing here is, unless they know this little trick then they will undermine themselves, because they stare harder at your eyes which in some instances will produce a very light hypnoidial state which undermines their assertiveness and leads them to invariably end up backing down. The advantage becomes a psychological one whereby they, having blinked first, engender a sense that they have backed down from your will. This gives you the edge in your conversations or negotiations with them.

Another trick, when in a difficult situation, is to imagine that you are surrounded by a brilliant aura. A bubble of razor sharp steel through which nothing can penetrate, you can even let it send back to the sender that which they are intending you.

A silent intoning of perhaps a few lines from the *Book of Jeremiah* 21:11 is also effective:

> 'The Lord is with me as a mighty and terrible one, therefore my persecutors shall stumble and they shall not prevail.'

Such lines as these will help to concentrate the mind and will re-enforce the workings for a greater effect.

The regular use of the Lesser Banishing Ritual of the Pentagram , with the performing of the Middle Pillar exercise will help maintain a healthy auric field. This is no bad thing to do anyway, as the benefits will become apparent on several levels once regularity with this simple, but effective, practice has been established.

Sometimes, atmospheres in homes or buildings can be oppressive or can feed a run of bad luck. Practices such as leaving an onion that has been cut in half in a room overnight and then burning it, have always been a traditional trick to clear bad vibes. So has also leaving a dish of vinegar in a room overnight and then disposing of it away from the property.

Another method of quietening a house or building would to be to perform the Lesser Banishing Ritual of the Pentagram whilst burning a little frankincense and benzoin resin, or using the herb loosestrife as a sole incense. Visualise the pentagrams forming close to you and then let them move out to the very boundaries of the building, pushing back all negativity. With the formation of the figures at the compass points see them as tall and terrible, facing out and armed with drawn swords to turn back any hostility.

The sprinkling of all rooms with the waters of our arte will help to dispel disquietening entities and so will the censing of all rooms. Naturally both these actions will have to be done with intent and a form of words that encompasses your aims will also be necessary. When done, return to the centre point of your operations and as nature abhors a vacuum then it is best not to leave one. Visualise, from upon high, that the whole building is being flooded with a white divine brilliance. Let this light bring peace and harmony in its wake to all those who dwell in the home or building that you are working on. The use of an appropriate *psalm* would be a good idea too, such as *Psalm 30* for instance, or a form of words of your choosing that sums up your intent. If it was felt relevant then a full scale ritual working, invoking the powers of the Sun in its aspects of promoting harmony, peace and goodwill to all those who dwell therein, would certainly be something to consider.

As said before occult attacks on the individual are rare, but not unknown and, as the twentieth century magician Dion Fortune said, *'For forged notes to be accepted then the Bank of England has to issue real ones'*. In other words there must be real hauntings and occult attacks in existence and it is distinguishing between the real and the unreal that is the nub of the matter; which some people seem unable to do. Therefore it is inevitable that they will blame everything that goes wrong on the workings of those who they perceive are against them, instead of doing something positive to improve their situation themselves. For them to do so would be an act of real magic.

CHAPTER EIGHT

'I can call spirits from the vasty deep'

Glyndwr: 'I can call spirits from the vasty deep'
Hotspur: 'Why so can I, so can any man;
But will they come when you do call them?'

Shakespeare Henry IV, Part I

This is everyone's image of the sorcerer/ess, the being who can command the entities of the other worlds and who has an invisible army at their back to do their will. Up to a point this can be so, but not everything is bendable, and, as said before, to approach the intelligences and spirits of both the elements and the planets is not to be done lightly, as some of these *'critters can bite.'* To approach this work, rightly called evocation, you will need to have mastered, or at least be familiar and able to get success with, all the work that we have covered so far. As the name says, evocation means *'to call forth'*, but where from? Whether you want to take a Jungian attitude and suggest that the spirits are energies that reside in your subconscious, or consider that they are completely separate from you and have their own separate plane of existence is not important, because they exist.

On their own levels and in the worlds where divinity has placed them, they are real as you and I. The fact that they can be summoned forth and that they can wreak effects on the physical levels is true, regardless of the opinions of unbelievers in such phenomena.

The inhabitants of the spirit worlds can, by the skills and demands of our artes, be evoked to visible appearance into the speculum (the magical mirror, or crystal). They can also be called to a specially consecrated triangle outside your circle wherein they are manifested and where they can be politely, but firmly, induced to perform your will, providing it is within the bounds of their office. As I have not had the experience of summoning to physical appearance into the triangle of arte, other than one act of sciomancy , the summoning of the shades of the dead, I am unable to write of such things, but I have had several experiences of successful evocation of spirits into the speculum. The first thing is that they may not appear as tradition decrees, but on instruction and by the invoking of the holy names that control them, they can and will adopt a more pleasing appearance.

During one evocation sometime ago involving the elemental king of water, Niksa, I was shown what I thought was an incredible vision of the working of water in the world. It involved the formation of rain clouds and the releasing of the rain on to the dry land. In particular, one drop of the rain was shown me, which stood out from the rest that was falling. I watched as it hit the ground and was absorbed. I could see the water droplet, which seemed to have a life that was its own, with an intelligence that animated it, dissolve and soak up the nutrients in the soil. The thirsty roots of a nearby plant sucked up this life-giving force and as the moisture evaporated from the leaves, I was made aware, as I had never been before, that nature abhorred a vacuum. So as the moisture evaporated at the one end it was sucked in at the other, just like a pump. The evaporated water went off into the atmosphere and eventually formed more rain clouds, which performed the same operation again and again. The vision in the speculum was as clear as day and with a vibrancy that was all its own. Did I delude myself? No, I don't feel that I did. Was it real? For me it was and that, for me, was the important thing. You will have your own experiences so you must be your own judge.

One method of creating effects on the physical and mental levels is the summoning forth of elemental energies and the creation of an elemental or servitor. These beings can be created for a specific reason and to work within a narrow field of operation relevant to the element's nature. For example, a servitor based on the element water would be useful in influencing an emotional matter, whilst fire would be the natural choice for the protection or destruction of a building or person. The problem is that these beings, although extremely useful, must have a set time to exist and then must be destroyed. If not, they can get out of hand and the destruction of them will become more difficult.

There are several ways in which these beings can be birthed and we will consider a simple but effective way. Firstly it is a good thing to have a physical body for your servitor and a name for it. The physical body could be a doll or statue of some sort, or even a stone. Set up the circle of arte relevant to the element that is suitable to the work. Use an invocation of your own devising to the element concerned. Consecrate and dedicate the physical form that will house the energies summoned forth, using the holy waters and suffumigations of our arte.

Give it a name at this point and anoint it with some of the elemental fluid condenser, which will greatly improve the capacity of the physical body to hold the energies that are summoned. If you can insert some inside the body it will be all to the good, or paint the statue (or whatever it is that you are using) with the elemental fluid condenser. Place the body that is being used inside your circle at the edge , let it be in the right elemental quarter too. If the work is for yourself I would suggest that you use the Middle Pillar exercise and flood your aura with the appropriate colours and names of power that are suitable to the work in hand. Now taking your wand, pour out all the energies into the figure before you. Let the energies summoned appear as a figure of your own devising. For example they can be as a huge warrior if the servitor is one of protection.

Now you must instruct it in its ways and duties. The instructions must be clear and must not be of an ambiguous nature. Set the length of its life such as 'until the full of the next Moon, whenst thou will return unto that from which thou hast come', or a year and a day, whatever is needed. At the end of its life a new servitor can be brought forth to carry on the work. You must see the physical body before you, that is to house the energies aroused, absorb the power brought forth. As the power is absorbed by the physical body of the servitor do not think that becasue the power has been taken into a smaller form, that the ability of it has been diminished. The servitor must be kept somewhere safe and secret. Do not let anyone know its name, as they could gain control over it.

To destroy it, you must see it before you and you must call it by name. Thank it for the work that it has done and command it to go back whence it came. See it shrink and fade away and feel the energies being reabsorbed by the element that it came from. The physical form that housed the body can be buried to let the earth cleanse any energies still clinging to it. Alternatively you can leave it in running water with the intent that anything still there is now being cleansed.

If you are creating a servitor for someone else, then do not charge it with energies that are brought into being via the Middle Pillar, as these will, if you are not careful, leave you open to being affected by the creature and the individual that it has been created for. Instead, imagine the energies gathering around the figure before you and see, as you did before, the energies take on a form of an appropriate shape, which should then be instructed in its duties. When you feel that the energies are as strong as you can muster and are sated with your intent let them sink down into the physical body that is to house them.

With such workings it may be necessary to repeat the operation more than once, but that will be dependent on the nature of the problem, and how much energy you have called forth.

Evocation of spirits:

If you do not have a magical mirror for this work then you will have to construct one. One method is to use a bowl and pour into it some of the fluid condenser and darken it with some black ink. This, whilst simple, will work well. To make first of all a mirror suitable for our arte, unless you are using a crystal, hunt down from somewhere the glass of a clock face. Having washed it clean, you must paint the inside with black paint and with some of the fluid condenser. Use the universal condenser rather than one of the elemental ones.

As the speculum is a passive tool and one of reflection consecrate it within a circle of arte that invokes the lunar powers. Within this circle summon the powers of the Moon, consecrate and dedicate it accordingly. Afterwards let the mirror be placed outside and under the Moon to soak up the powers thereof. The next morning get up early and retrieve the mirror before sunrise. Then the mirror must be wrapped in a clean cloth, silk would be ideal for this, and must be put away out of daylight and the view of the profane.

Evocation:

Decide which planet best suits the purpose of the work, and then prepare everything so that you start the working during the relevant planetary hour of the planetary day. With this working you will do better if you have fasted for several hours beforehand. Some authorities will insist that you fast for several days, however it is your will that brings success to pass not an empty stomach. Having said that fasting does heighten the psychic senses, so do not try this on a full stomach as you will need all your psychic wits about you.

Clean thoroughly your workspace, you must also be thoroughly clean as well. Make sure that you have everything that you will need and that your bladder is not full, as you must stay within your circle until the working is finished. When all is gathered together and you are ready, contemplate the work in hand, a prayer for the success of the work would be no bad thing. When you are ready, cast your circle of arte. Draw in the appropriate coloured inks the sigil of the planetary spirit on a square of parchment.

On the back draw the planetary seal. This sigil must now be consecrated to the success of the work. Name it with the spirit's name and treat it as such. Place the mirror on the altar top with the sigil under the mirror. Trace on the mirror with your finger, dipped in some of the fluid condenser, the sigil of the spirit. Take a white cord and lay it around the mirror as an equilateral triangle. The boundary of this triangle must be consecrated with fire and water, saying:

> 'In and by the Holy Names of God, I do conjure thee O Triangle of Arte,
> to constrain and hold the energies that I do evoke into thee.
> Wherefore I do bless, dedicate and consecrate thee to this end.
> So Mote it Be!'

Take the athana and pointing it at the triangle boundary, visualise pouring from its point, a stream of white brilliance. Let this light travel around the edge of the triangle in a clockwise fashion and see it as a shimmering wall over which nothing can cross.

Keep the censer going and use an invocation such as *'Blessed art thou etc'*, then the *'Ol Sonuf Vaorsagi'* etc and *'I invoke thee thou angels of the celestial spheres'* etc invocations.

Anoint your head with the Abra-Melin oil. This can be bought or made, and consists of the oils of cinnamon, galangal and myrrh. This oil is considered extremely holy and is first found in the 14th century work, *The Abra-Melin*.

Use the Middle Pillar exercise and flood your aura with a brilliant white light. Endeavour to identify with the energies that are aroused. You must spend a little time contemplating the imagery and the attributes thereof. Now crossing your arms over your chest, concentrate on a shining and dazzling white sphere above your head and declare the ancient words of hallowing that are instrumental in promoting your authority:

> 'I am he, the bornless spirit
> having sight in the feet: strong and the immortal fire.

I am he the truth.
I am he, who hates that evil should be wrought in the world.
I am he, who lighteneth and thundereth.
I am he, from whom is the shower of life of earth.
I am He, Whose mouth ever flameth:
I am he, the Begetter and the Manifester unto the Light.
I am he, the Grace of the World.
The Heart girt with a Serpent is my Name'.
'Come thou forth and follow me and make all spirits subject unto me, so that every spirit of the firmament and of the ether,
upon the earth and under the earth, on dry land and in the water, of whirling air and of rushing fire and every spell and scourge of God the vast and mighty one may be made obedient unto me.
IAO SABAO (ee-ah-oh sah-bah-oh) such are the words'.

Now, walking clockwise around your circle, ensuring that you do not break the boundary line and starting in the east, declare to the element at each quarter your work. Return to the centre and face east. This work will stamp your authority on the following operation and, owing to the link that you have with divinity, which has just been reinforced, you are now ready to proceed.

Visualise that your aura is filling up with the coloured light that is relevant to the work in hand, in this case gold, as we are working with solar spirits in this example.

Intone firmly and solemnly the God name and the Archangel name relevant to the working in hand and, with your wand (not the fire wand), trace in the air before you the invoking hexagram of the Sun.

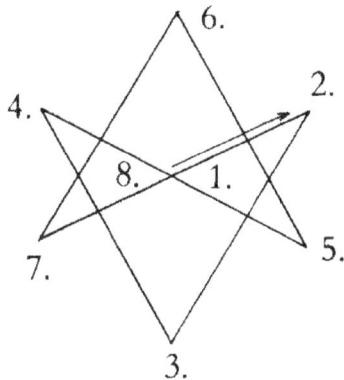

See the mirror flooded with the colour relevant to the work. This helps to create an atmosphere sympathetic to the spirit.

Use a solar invocation general to the work in hand and then exclaim:

'Sorath! Sorath! Sorath! Hear me!
For I do evoke thee
by the mighty and the potent names of God YHVH ALOAH
VA DAATH!
and by the power of the Holy Archangel MIKAEL!
And by the might of the Malakim
and by the solar intelligence Nakiel,
to appear in this mirror of arte within this triangle, here
upon this holy altar.
Come in peace and come by the holy name YHVH ALOAH
VA DAATH!
Come in a comely form!
Come speaking words of truth and of understanding!'

Gaze into the mirror, the mirror may shift out of focus and come back again. This is normal. Wait a little while and scenes will appear. The spirit will take on a form if commanded by the holy names to do so. The communications that take place will be by visions in the mirror or by conversations that take place in your head. This I accept will sound strange but it is the best way that I can think of to explain it. You will get the sense that the ideas are from outside you. Do not doubt that this is happening, as you may damage the link between you and the spirit. You may at this point instruct the spirit in its duties, but remember that they must be within the spirit's field of expertise. If the spirit has not appeared after the first evocation, then repeat it.

This may be repeated up to three times in all. If the spirit still has not appeared then trace the solar hexagram again, but this time use the sword, and holding the sword in your right hand, with the wand in your left hand use the following evocation:

'I invoke and move thee, O thou Spirit X
and being exalted above thee in the power of the Most
High, I command thee Obey!
In the names Beralanensis, Baldachiensis, Paumachia and
Apologiae Sedes.
By the most powerful Princes, Genii, Liachidae and ministers
of the Tartarean Abode
and by the chief Prince of the Seat of Apologia in the Ninth
Legion.

I do invoke thee and by invoking thee, I do conjure thee!
I, who being exalted above ye in the powers of the Most High, do say unto thee,
Obey!
By the name of him who spoke
and it was and unto whom all creatures do obey.'
'Furthermore,
I who art made by God in the likeness thereof do stir thee up!
Come thou now forth and make manifest within this mirror that abides within this triangle of arte that is before me!
Hear me and come thou forth! Come thou forth, I do command thee by the mighty and the holy names of God the Vast and Mighty One!
ADONAI, EL, ELOHIM, ELOHI, EHYEH ASHER EHYEH, ZABAOTH, ELION, IAH, TETRAGRAMMATON, SHADDAI, LORD GOD MOST HIGH!'

Now gaze into the mirror and see. Greet the spirit in the God names and the name of the archangelic force that governs the work in hand. When the spirit has answered your questions and has agreed to your commands then license it to depart. This is very important as the forces brought forth must return unto whence they came.

License to Depart:

Trace in the air over the altar with your sword, the banishing hexagram of the planet that governs the work (in this case the Sun) and see the energies fade away.

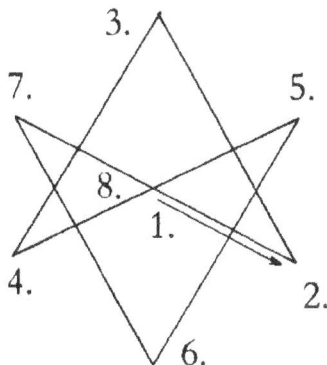

The banishing hexagram of the Sun

Declaring:

> 'In and by the mighty and the holy names YHVH ALOAH VA
> DAATH
> and by the power of the archangel Mikael
> and by the might of the Malakim
> and by thine intelligence Nakiel,
> I do, O Sorath give thee license to depart unto thine proper
> abodes and habitations.
> Go therefore in peace
> and let there be grace and goodwill between thee and me
> now and for always, for I too am a servant of the God Most
> High!
> So Mote It Be!'

Still facing the eastern quarter say *'Non Nobis Domini Non Nobis'* etc. Re-consecrate your circle with fire and water and close with the Lesser Banishing Ritual of the Pentagram, but this time banish with the banishing pentagram that is relevant to each quarter.

Say:

> 'I now set free any spirits
> that have be constrained by the ritual,
> go in peace unto thine proper places
> and go with the blessings of the God Most High!'

After the ritual, I suggest that you get something to eat and drink, partly because you are probably hungry but also to shut down from the work that has just taken place. Put everything away and keep the spirit's sigil out of sight. When the work has come to fruition then the sigil can be destroyed.

Another working, which I have included here under evocation, is the use of the demonic seals from the *Lesser Key of Solomon*, the *Goetia*. Whilst we are not evoking them to physical appearance via the triangle or speculum, I am including them under evocation because that, because of their nature, is where they rightly belong. In the *Goetia*, pronounced Go-ee-sha, there are seventy-two spirits, which all, legend says, escaped from King Solomon's control. They all have a specific field of influence and I have found, from experience, that one can consecrate the seal of the spirit and by placing it in the consecrated triangle of arte, outside the circle, it can be treated as the spirit and used to produce effects in the physical world.

There are also seventy-two angels, one for each Goetic spirit, whose seal must be drawn on the back of the parchment that has the Goetic spirit's sigil on. There is also a Latin invocation that goes with each angel and that also must be written on the back of the sigil. This invocation must also be recited. Of the seventy-two spirits, I have given seven here, together with their governing angels and the angel's invocations and sigils. I have adapted the angelic invocations and sigils from *The Book of Solomon's Magick* by Carroll 'Poke' Runyon and from the Harley manuscript 6482 in the British Library. Further information can be found from both these sources.

Vassago:

His office is to declare things past and to come. He discovers all things lost or hidden. To be worked with during the hour of Jupiter.

Incense: Cedar

Sigil of Vassago in blue:

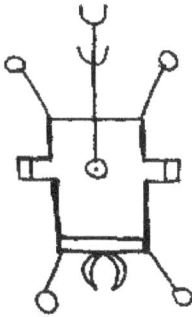

Sigil of Governing Angel Sitael:

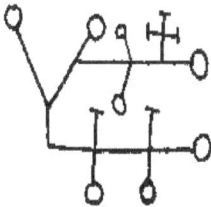

Invocation of the Governing Angel Sitael:

> *'Dicam Domino susceptor meus estu, et refugium meum*
> *Deus meus sperabo in sum: Sitael.'*

'I shall say to the Lord, thou art my guardian, my God is my refuge and I shall hope in him.'

Gusion:

Shows the future, grants honours and dignities, and reconciles enemies.

Incense: rose

Sigil of Gusion in green:

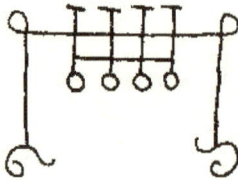

Sigil of Governing Angel Lauiah:

Invocation of Governing Angel Lauiah:

'Vivit Domininus et benedictus Deus meus et exaltetur Deus salutis meae: Lauiah.'

'The Lord liveth, blessed is my God and let the God of my salvation be exalted.'

Foras:

Teaches the powers and properties of herbs and stones. Will help to find things that are lost.

Incense: lavender

Seal of Foras in orange:

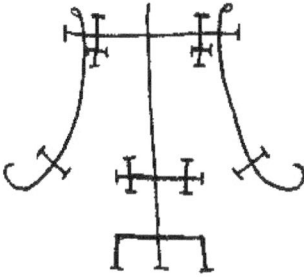

Sigil of Governing Angel Lecabel:

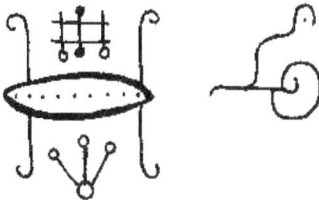

Invocation of Governing Angel Lecabel:

'Introibo in potentia Domini,
Deus meus memorabor iustitiae tuae solius: Lecabel.'

'I shall enter into the power of the Lord my God I shall be
mindful of thy justice only.'

Uvall:

His office is to promote the love between man and woman. He will also promote friendship between people. He also has knowledge of the past, present and the future.

Incense: rose

Seal of Uvall in green:

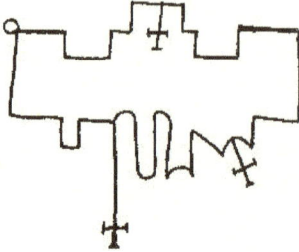

Sigil of Governing Angel Asaliah:

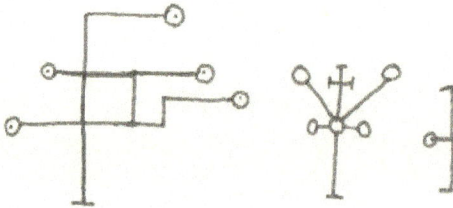

Invocation of Governing Angel Asaliah:

'Quam magnificata sunt opera tua Domini,
nimis profundae factae sunt cogitations tuae: Asaliah.'

'How wonderful are thy works, O Lord and how deep thy thoughts.'

Orobas:

Will grant favours and goodwill from those who are in authority. He also will promote the favour of friends and foes and will reveal things past, present and to come.

Incense: cedar

Seal of Orobas in blue:

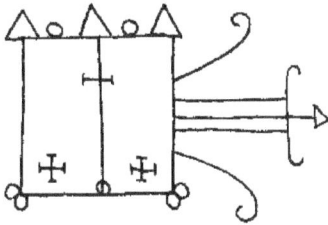

Sigil of Governing Angel Mebahiah:

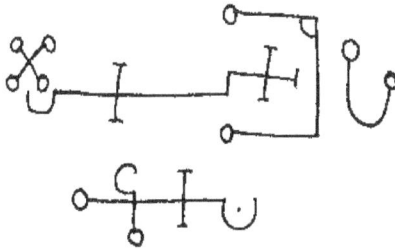

Invocation of Governing Angel Mebahiah:

'Tu autem Domine in aeternum permanes et memoriale tuum in generationem et generationem: Mebahiah.'

'Thou remainest for ever, O Lord
and thy memorial is from generation unto generation.'

Oriax:

Teaches astrology, promotes friendships and the favour of those who can help the sorcerer/ess.

Incense: jasmine

Seal of Oriax in purple:

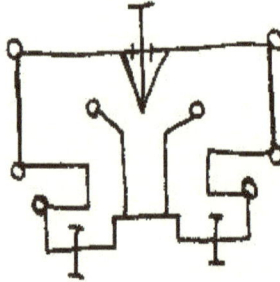

Sigil of Governing Angel Harachel:

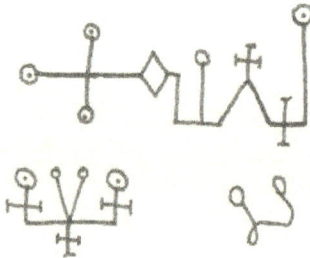

Invocation of Governing Angel Harachel:

'Ab ortu Solis usque ad occasum laudabile nomen Domini: Harachel.'

'From the rising of the Sun to the going down of the same, The word of the Lord is worthy of praise.'

Dantalion:

Will reveal other peoples' secrets. He knows exactly what is going on in other peoples' lives. Can promote love and friendship.

Incense: rose

Seal of Dantalion in green:

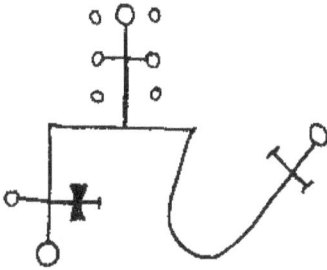

Sigil of Governing Angel Haiael:

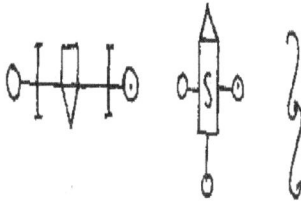

Invocation of Governing Angel Haiaiel:

'Confitebor Domino nimis in ore meo
et in medio multorum laudabo eum Haiaiel.'

'I shall confess to the Lord with my mouth and praise him in the midst of the multitude.'

Of the Triangle of Arte:

The triangle of arte is depicted in the *Key of Solomon* thus and has been used for centuries in sorcery as a means of controlling entities from the other planes.

In this instance it must be placed in the East outside your circle of the arte.

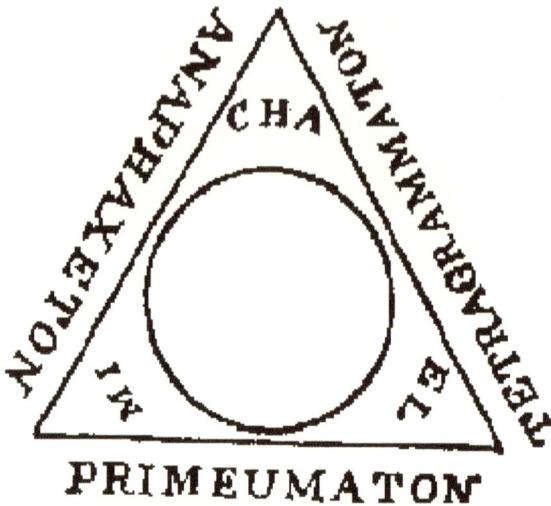

The triangle is an equilateral one and is drawn in chalk or in paint, with the names around it being written along its edge on the outside. The exception is the name of the archangel Mikael, which is written on the inside, as shown, preferably in red.

For this operation, let us assume that you have cleansed your working area and have gathered all your materials together. Perform the Lesser Banishing Ritual of the Pentagram and make sure that it has encompassed the area wherein your triangle now dwells. Prior to this you will have drawn your Goetic talismanic seal in the appropriate colour on parchment. On the back of it, you will have also drawn the angelic sigil and have written out on it the relevant Latin invocation for the angel concerned.

The talisman must now be consecrated with the waters of our arte in the manner that you will have become familiar with by now. Holding it in the rising incense smoke, say that this talisman is the seal of the spirit in question, who will bring about that which you are working for. Anoint it with the oil of Abra-Melin, the holy oil of our arte and the perfumed oil of your undaunted will. Invoke the controlling angelic force by reciting the Latin invocation and requesting the angel to assist in the operation.

The talisman must now be placed within the triangle, and, taking the chalice, sprinkle the boundary of the triangle in a clockwise manner with the holy waters of the arte, likewise consecrate the triangle with the censer. With both operations declare that you are consecrating the triangle by the powers of your divinity and by the holy names that are written there around and that the triangle will contain the energies that are aroused therein. Taking your sword and pointing it at the periphery of the triangle, see that a blast of divine brilliance pours forth and again trace the boundary of the triangle. Let this be done in the firm and certain knowledge that the energies summoned therein are subject to your will.

Around the edge of your circle write at the compass points the names of God relevant to each quarter. These can be the ones from the Lesser Banishing Ritual of the Pentagram and can be written in the Theban script.

Consecrate the circle of arte as previously taught and using the *'Blessed art thou'* invocation or one of your own devising invoke divinity. Proclaim the *'Ol Sonuf Vaorsagi'* and the *'I invoke thee, thou angels of the celestial spheres'* invocations. Also useful here is *Psalm 91*. Anoint your head with the oil of Abra-Melin and perform the Middle Pillar exercise. Let the whole of your being be flooded with the brilliance of your divinity. Use as you have before the Bornless invocation. Now with your sword in your left hand and your wand in your right declare your intent.

Again invoke the angel who governs the spirit that you are working with, using the Latin invocation that has been given, which you have written on the back of the talisman. Now, using a variant of the Goetic conjurations, which I give below, proceed thus.

Point your wand at the talismanic seal that is within the triangle and declare:

> *'I invoke thee and thy powers O Spirit X,*
> *and being armed with power from the Supreme Majesty,*
> *I do strongly command thee by Beralanensis, Baldachiensis,*
> *Paumachia and Apologiae Sedes,*

> *by the most powerful princes, genii, liachidae and ministers*
> *of the Tartarean abode*
> *and by the Chief Prince of the Seat of Apologia in the Ninth*
> *Legion, I do invoke thy holy powers to consecrate the*
> *talisman within the circle of arte to (state the aim of the*
> *work) which is my will!*
> *Furthermore, being armed with power from the Supreme*
> *Majesty,*
> *I do strongly command thee by him who spake and it was*
> *done and unto whom all creatures obey*
> *and I who art made in the image of God, endowed with*
> *power from God and created according unto his will*
> *I do command thee by that most mighty and powerful*
> *name of God EL strong and wonderful!*
> *O Spirit X, I do command thee by all the names of God and*
> *by the names Adonai, El, Elohim, Elohi, Ehyeh Asher Ehyeh,*
> *Zabaoth, Elion, Iah,*
> *Tetragrammaton, Shaddai, Lord God Most High, to fulfil my*
> *commands and persist thou therein unto the end according*
> *unto my interest.*
> *So Mote It Be!'*

See in the triangle a ball of coloured light that is the same as the colour of the spirit's sigil on the talisman. Look into the ball of light and see your will being accomplished and let the light be absorbed by the talisman.

Do not visualise any of the spirit's traditional forms, as you do not need a manifestation. In your own wording give thanks to divinity and use the following as the License to Depart:

> *'I do thank thee O Spirit X for attending unto my will, which*
> *thou wilt make manifest as I have decreed.*
> *Furthermore, I do license thee to depart by the names of the*
> *God Most High.*
> *Go therefore in peace*
> *unto thy proper abodes and habitation,*
> *Let there be peace, grace and harmony between thee and*
> *me now and for always.*
> *So Mote It Be!'*

Re-consecrate the circle of the arte with fire and water. Use the *'Non Nobis'* wording of thanks too. Banish with the Lesser Banishing Ritual of the Pentagram and use the correct elemental pentagram at the right quarter. Declare that any spirits that have been invoked are released from this ritual unto their proper places and say:

'Domine Unam Est

The Lord is One'

Take the talisman out of the triangle and cover it up, but not with a silk cloth, as this will interfere with its efficiency. It must now be placed somewhere safe and left undisturbed to do your will.

Necromancy:

In the Middle Ages, a necromancer would have been someone who worked magic and not simply someone who evoked the dead, which we interpret the word as meaning today. It is often considered that the dead are to be left alone and that no good will come of your trafficking with them. However, in my limited experience I would disagree with this. Mediums and the spiritualists of this world are frequently in communication with the dead, which suggests to me that they don't, on the whole, mind a little interaction with those of this world. There are two rituals that I am aware of for evoking the dead: one is from the work of Paul Huson, *Mastering Witchcraft* and the other from another source.

Evocation of the dead, that is the summoning of the person's shade into the triangle of the arte, is no easy operation and from my own experience it may not work out as you expected. In my own case, one All Hallows Eve, several years ago, I set out to evoke the shade of my old friend and occult teacher who had died many years ago. Seeing that she had been cremated and her ashes scattered in her garden, in the same street that I was living in at the time, I thought that she wouldn't have far to come. Anyway, All Hallows Eve in this particular year in question fell exactly at the dark of the Moon, an ideal time for contacting the dead.

So I set to work. For thirteen nights previously at midnight I had entered my workspace and there enkindled some incense and placed a photograph of her on the altar between two candles. Here I had spent some time concentrating on her and our past associations. Thinking about this working in the daytime is completely different to doing it at midnight, so expect the hairs on the back of your head to stand up occasionally! This constant calling at this time of night and the burning of a little incense will help to establish that subtle link that is needed for the success of the work. On the fourteenth day, All Hallows Eve, I fasted and cleaned the area of operations thoroughly. In the evening with a clean black altar cloth and two unused black candles, consecrated to our arte, I set to work. The operation was timed to start at midnight. However, about an hour before the work started I became assailed with all manner of fears and doubts, and started to talk myself out of doing the ritual. It did, I must confess, take some doing to get back up and see the work through and I did say to myself that if I didn't go through with it and make a success of it, then I was finished as far as magic was concerned. Although I did point out to myself that by going through with the planned operation, then life wouldn't be exactly the same again.

Having pulled myself together and fortified my undaunted will, I proceeded with the work. Being washed and suitably attired, I awaited the striking of the church clock to announce midnight. The triangle of arte was in the west, where I had placed the photo of the dead witch, and the whole operation was directed to that quarter. At the height of the ritual all light was extinguished and my gaze was on the triangle of the arte. What did I expect to see? Could it be done? Could a dead witch be called back momentarily? Well firstly, I hardly expected that she would appear in her old heavy black cloak, wearing her glasses on the end of her nose and quaffing a large glass of her favourite red wine, but then I wasn't expecting an angelic figure to appear either. So what happened? Well I can say there was no solid figure, as such, in the triangle. Was there a presence or not? One minute I thought there was, the next I wasn't sure.

Apart from the incredible atmosphere that was present, the only phenomena that I was sure of was the presence of the room spinning and the lights that flashed about the circle's edge. Was this psychic phenomena or simply me being disorientated? But what did happen was rather curious and didn't take place until the following All Hallows Eve. It was during the day of this festival that I walked around the corner and into the street where the dead witch used to live - standing outside her old house was one of her sons, who I had not seen for some twenty years. Although I recognised him he was not quite sure of me, but before I could say anything he said in a voice, that even today I am convinced sounded exactly like his mother's, *'Remember me to Gary'* then walked off, before I could say anything in reply. Was this simply a coincidence or was it the magic making manifest in a way that I hadn't expected it to do? The chances of me being in that place at that time, the anniversary of the working, outside the old witch's house and meeting her son, were, I felt, remote.

The message he gave me, which I am still certain was in his mother's voice, so unlike his own, I found to be extremely appropriate. However, that which I wanted to ask her, at the necromantic working previously, I found out from another source, some weeks after the working. Whilst I wouldn't say that this operation was an outstanding success I couldn't say it was a failure either. I do think that the lack of direction and temporary confusion and fear I felt an hour or so before the start of the ritual would have robbed the working of some of the power that I had been carefully building up over the previous thirteen nights. So once again, I can only reiterate that once you start a piece of magical work then you must see it through, you cannot waver and then expect success. Magic is a hard discipline and there can be no half measures if you want your work to be successful.

With necromancy the working must be orientated to the west; your triangle of arte needs to be in the west. This is appropriate, seeing that the Sun goes down in the west. This work is best performed on one of the nights just before the new Moon; naturally the altar cloth and candles need to be black.

A suitable incense such as the following traditional one is to be used: on a waning Moon take equal amounts of the following herbs and resins: church incense, wormwood, dittany of Crete and gum mastic, to this add a few drops of olive oil and a little of your lifeblood. Mix well and store safely.

Fasting for necromantic working is essential, as you will need to be psychically aware for this work. For thirteen nights before the night that you are going to perform your necromantic working, take a photo of the deceased into your working space. Set it up between two new candles and burn a little of the necromantic incense. Spend some time in contemplation of the deceased and explain what it is that you are about. If you do not have a photo to hand, then I would suggest that you draw a sigil of their name, not on a planetary square but by combining the letters of their name as shown earlier.

On the night of the working, being suitably prepared according to the rules of our arte, and wearing the pentacle of protection, enter your workspace and give prayer for the success of the work in hand. Kindle the incense and the lights.

Firstly use the Lesser Banishing Ritual of the Pentagram to clear the area and in the west draw the triangle of arte as previously shown. Then place therein the photo or the sigil of the deceased which has been consecrated, named and identified thus: firstly it is to be consecrated with fire and water and then with your wand trace a circle in blue wherein is an equal-armed cross.

Saying as you do:

> *'Colpriziana Offina Alta Nestera Fuaro Menut I name thee X*
> *For thou art X'*

This triangle must be hallowed with fire and water and by the power of your sword. Cast your circle and invoke the compass points as you have been shown elsewhere. Use the invocations *'Blessed art thou'* etc; *'Ol Sonuf Vaorsagi'* etc; and *'I invoke thee thou angels of the celestial spheres'* etc.

Whilst the deceased is not governed by planetary considerations, as are the spirits that are generally evoked in evocation, you would do well to invoke your own divinity, via the Middle Pillar exercise, to add poise and potency to your working.

Approach the eastern quarter and raise your wand high saying:

'O spirit of X, ye who art deceased, Hear me!
For thou mayest approach the gates of the east to answer
truly my demands.
Berald, Beroald, Balbin Gab, Gabor, Agaba!
Arise for I do command thee!'

Walking backwards go to the south and repeat, then do this for the west and the northern quarters. Now you must go to the east of the altar and face the western quarter wherein resides your triangle of arte. Maintain a silence for a short while and stoking up the thurible with the incense, proceed. Point your wand at the photo or sigil in the triangle of arte and declare:

'By the mysteries of the deep,
By the flames of Banal,
By the power of the east, and by the silence of the night,
By the holy rites of Hecate,
I do conjure thee and I do exorcise thee O spirit X!
That thou presenteth thy self here
And answer truly my demands of thee.
So Mote It Be!'

Put out all light at his point and plunge the room into darkness. Now you must carefully, and walking backwards, go to the west of the altar and there kneel down and face the triangle. Cross your arms over your breast and say:

'Allay Fortission Fortissio Allynsen, Roa'

Close your eyes and maintain a strict silence for a few moments. When you are ready and with your eyes still shut, greet the spirit silently and then as you extend your arms slowly into the shape of a cross say clearly and firmly the name of the deceased spirit. Open your eyes now and see what you see. Is the spirit there? Perhaps it is just a dim and faint figure, or maybe a full manifestation that leaves you in no doubt.

Others may just experience a strong presence of the person summoned.

However the manifestation takes place, ask your question at this point, or what it is that you want from the dead because surely you have not been foolish enough to summon them from their rest for your own idle curiosity.

When the form fades trace your steps back to the altar and rekindle the lights. Place more incense on the thurible and repeat the License to Depart:

> 'Go departed shade of X, Omgroma Epin Sayoc,
> Satony, Degony, Eparigon Galiganon, Zogogen, Ferstigon.
> For I do license thee to depart unto thy proper abodes and
> habitations
> Go in peace and let there be harmony
> between us now and for evermore.
> So Mote It Be!'

Reconsecrate the circle of arte with fire and water and give thanks for the success of your working. Close with a thorough banishing and put the photo or sigil somewhere safe. Now close down with some hot food and drink. It could very well be that the shade of the person evoked may come through to you in your dreams that night, or the answer that you seek may be shown to you in the next few weeks by someone or an event that happens to you. By whatever means the answer comes to you - and it will - then take note.

The Pentacle of Protection:

This device is taken from the medieval text *The Lesser Key of Solomon*. It is a consecrated symbol that grants protection and success in the rites of evocation and has become an essential piece of the armoury of the sorcerer/ess. For its construction take, on the Tuesday before the full Moon, a square of parchment and draw upon it the following symbols in red ink, in which you have added a few drops of your Universal Fluid Condenser and a couple of drops of your blood.

Setting up the circle of arte as you have been instructed, burn a little church incense in which you have added a small amount of dragon's blood. Let the symbol be consecrated and dedicated with fire and water, that it will preserve and protect you from all hostility whilst you are engaged in the arte magical. It would be useful to use *Psalm 91* in this working, as the wording certainly captures the essence of what this particular work is about.

When you have consecrated the pentacle, wrap it up in a clean cloth (silk would be preferable) and wear it, suspended on a red thread, from your neck with the pentacle being uncovered so that it is displayed on your chest. This symbol only needs to be used during works of evocation and is not needed for general magical workings. The circle of arte is banished in the usual manner.

Hexagrams:

These symbols are used in the invocation and evocation of planetary energies and are traced in the air and visualised in the planetary colours relevant to the working, with the planet's symbol seen in the centre of the hexagram. Each angle of the hexagram has a planet associated with it; the Sun is in the centre. To invoke you draw the first line to the planet's angle; draw it away from the angle to banish it.

Saturn

Invoking Saturn

Banishing Saturn

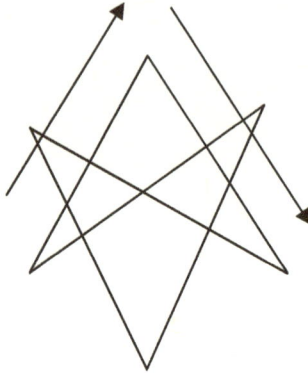

The Hexagram with planetary associations:

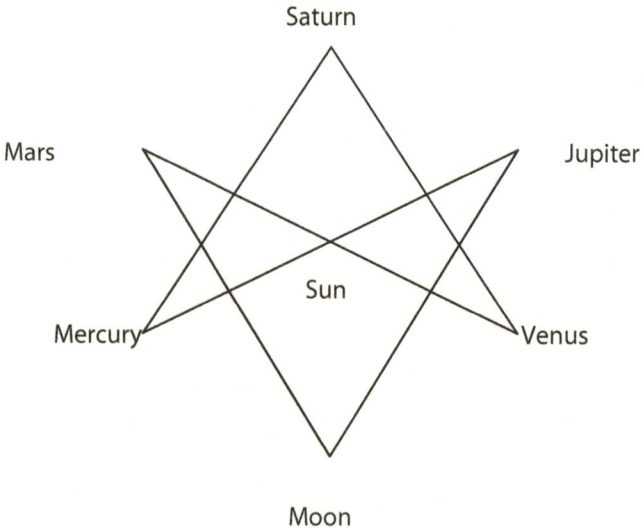

Saturn

Mars

Jupiter

Sun

Mercury

Venus

Moon

CHAPTER NINE

'Myself made perfect whom no man hath seen'

With the pursuit of magic and the fruits thereof, it is easy to be less than mindful of the divine and, as you are busy going about your magical business, the whole concept of Divinity and your relationship therewith can easily take second place. Crowley's secretary, Israel Regardie, pointed out that magic and the development of the skills and attributes needed for the successful practicing thereof, were primarily, in some occult quarters, considered only to be used for contacting and exploring the subtle powers that had conceived and maintain creation; anything else was to be considered black magic. These days, however, I generally think that black magic is the thing that the other person does, not me.

Within the corpus of the Western Magical Tradition (by that, I do not include Wicca and New Age), is the concept of *'One's Higher Self'*, sometimes referred to as *'The Holy Guardian Angel.'* For some people this entity, this other you, and the conversation and contact thereof, becomes the primary purpose of their magical work. Anything else is of a secondary and inconsequential nature. This can be seen in the medieval occult grimoire *The Sacred Magic of Abra-Melin the Mage*. This work, whilst it can grant some remarkable powers, is extremely demanding, but it is highly regarded for the contacts it can promote with one's own Higher Self.

Crowley used a similar regimen with his opus *Liber Samekh*, where the celebrant withdraws for several months from the hurly-burly of life and goes on a thorough disciplined magical retreat, with a set ritual being performed at regular times throughout the day. This is performed for months on end at the end of which the goal of the work - the knowledge, and the contact and experiencing of your Higher Self - will, if you have *'enflamed yourself with prayer'* sufficiently, take place. With all the benefits that flow therefrom.

Whilst the present book is not a work that takes you specifically down that road, many of the skills that you develop and the experiences that you have from following it, will be of beneficial use in the promotion of the *'Knowledge and Conversation of your Higher Self'*.

One such working that will help to prepare you is the regular practice of the following Elemental Mass. This ritual has been devised from a variety of sources and is useful in balancing and developing an understanding of one's own elemental nature. It is a ritual that needs to be worked on a regular basis to gain any benefits from it. Daily practice would be ideal.

Whilst some of you may baulk at this, it can be done. I know this because I did it for months on end, summer and winter, although it meant rising at five-thirty am to get it worked before I cycled the six miles to work as a gardener. The workspace that I used for this operation was a large shed that I had built at the bottom of the garden, with very little appreciable heating. Believe me; it takes a determined soul to keep going. But the fruits that it gave birth to are still with me today. So it comes tried and tested. This ritual, like all good workings, has an inner and an outer form, with the outer being but a reflection of the inner. It is the inner which does the work, whilst the outer, being but the conscious form thereof, will reinforce it.

The Rite of On-Nophris:

Let the celebrant, being suitably washed, purified and clothed, approach the altar and let there be placed thereupon the elemental weapons of the arte. Let there also be upon the altar and in the eastern elemental quarter thereof, a bowl containing dried rose petals or better still a fresh rose (representing the element air). On the southern side of the altar place a lit red candle (fire) and on the western side thereof place a chalice containing a little wine (water). On the northern side of the altar place a small dish that contains bread and salt (earth). In the middle of the altar place the Abra-Melin oil (representing spirit). When all is ready enkindle the lights and some Abra-Melin incense. This is is composed of four parts olibanum, also known as frankincense, two parts lignum aloes and one part storax. If unavailable, use church incense.

1: Sprinkling thyself with the holy waters of our arte, better still if a sprig of hyssop can be used for an aspergillum, the celebrant declares:

> *'Asperges me Domine hyssopo*
> *Lavibis me super nivum et dealbabor'*

2: Perform the Lesser Banishing Ritual of the Pentagram and the consecrations of your space with fire and water.

3: Now hallow your working space with the summoning of the compass points.

4: Acknowledge and summon divinity with an invocation thereto, plus the 'Ol Sonuf Vaorsagi' and *'I invoke thee etc'* invocations.

5: Perform and construct the Middle Pillar within thee and when done concentrate upon a brilliant and blinding sphere above thy head and say:

> *'I invoke thee my higher self Thou who art with me for all*
> *time*
> *For I invoke thee my likeness and completion*
> *I invoke thee in whom I am made perfect and whole For in*
> *the dark and in the deeps*
> *Let the divine light of my being shine forth.'*

6: The celebrant of these mysteries, visualising and concentrating upon this sphere strives to place their conscious therein and to see the world therefrom. When sated with the effort, return to normal consciousness and there declare:

> *'I am He, the bornless spirit,*
> *having sight in the feet strong and the immortal fire.*
> *I am He, the truth*
> *I am He, who hateth that evil should be wrought in the*
> *world.*
> *I am He, who lighteneth and thundereth*
> *I am He, from who is the shower of the life of earth.*
> *I am He, the grace of the world*
> *I am He, Whose mouth ever flameth:*
> *I am He, the Begetter and Manifester unto the Light:*
> *That spirit who art made manifest within thee!'*

Now the celebrant sees their aura filling with the brilliance of their divinity and they state:'Let all malignancy and hindrance be cast forth hencefrom, so only the holy power of God may enter herein.

> *Wherefore, let me be blessed and made holy*

For I who art made in the image of God
Declare that I contain the very essence thereof.'

7: The celebrant pointing at the elements upon the altar says:

'Let these be as the elements of my body
Which is perfected through suffering and glorified through trial.
For the scent of the rose is but the expression of my suffering
Whilst the flame of the red fire is but the energy of my undaunted will.
With the holy cup of wine being the blood of my being, which I sacrifice unto regeneration and unto a newer life.
The bread and the salt, which is of the earth, is the foundation of my body, which is destroyed so that I may be renewed.
And the Holy Oil of Abra-Melin, which is but the glowing symbol of the spark that fell from upon high.
Hear me! O thou holy and potent powers of creation For thou art within me and I am but of thee!'

8: Now the celebrant being the Master of the Circle picketh up the rose and imbibes its perfume saying:

'Be thou prompt and active as the sylphs and not boastful nor squanderous'

Feeling the heat of the red flame with his hand says:

'To be brave and courageous as the salamanders but not cruel'

Drinking the wine the celebrant declareth:

'To be loving and giving as the undines
But not roused to jealousies'

Dipping the bread within the salt and eating, let the celebrant sayeth;

'Let me be as patient and steadfast as the gnomes
and not greedy,
So shalt I master the powers of the soul'

9: The celebrant, now having wettest the thumb of their right hand with the holy oil of Abra-Melin, they trace and visualise a glowing invoking pentagram upon their brow. Within the pentagram they trace and visualise a red Tau cross (T), upon which is encircled within its majesty, a winged, crowned and golden serpent. Let this symbol be the seal of the work and as this is done let them say:

'Accendat in nobis Adonia ignum sui amoris et flammam aeternae caritatis'

(let the Lord kindle in us the fire of his passion and the flame of his eternal love)

10: Now still facing east, the celebrant crosseth over their arms upon their breast and whilst visualising that they are crowned and ennobled within their glowing aura they intone firmly and victoriously the following invocation of triumph:

'Come thou forth and follow me and make all spirits subject unto me.
So that every spirit of the firmament and of the ether, upon the earth and under the earth.
Upon dry land and in the water,
Of whirling air and rushing fire.
And every spell and scourge of God the vast and the mighty one may be made obedient unto me!

IAO SABAO

(pronounced as ee-ah-oo-sah-bah-oh)

SUCH ART THE WORDS!'

11: Going to the eastern periphery of the circle of arte the celebrant gazeth into the far distance of the compass point and tracing the alchemical symbol for air in yellow before themselves they declare:

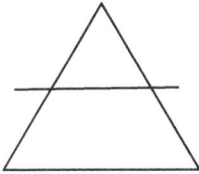

'In and by the holy names of God Shaddai El Chai and by the might of the holy archangel Raphael
and thine most potent angel Chassan and thy powerful king Paralda
Holy powers of element air
I do call thee forth to harmony
Let there be peace, grace and harmony between thee and me now and for always.
For I too am a servant of the God most high!'

Gazing into the eastern quarter the celebrant sees the holy powers of air and the works thereof.

12: They now travel to the southern quarter and the celebrant traces the alchemical symbol of fire in red.

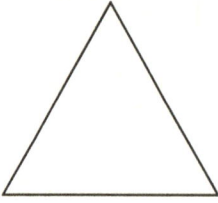

The celebrant repeateth the above formula but they do changeth the names and the visualisations accordingly.

God Name, *YHVH TZABAOTH*; Archangel, *Mikael*; Angel, *Aral*; King, *Djinn*

13: West, symbol in blue:

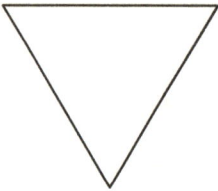

God Name, *Elohim Tzabaoth*; Archangel, *Gabriel*; Angel, *Taliahad*; King, *Niksha*

14: North: symbol in green:

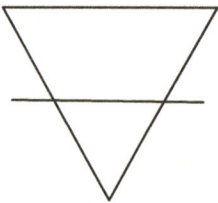

God Name, *Adonai Ha Aretz*; Archangel, *Auriel*; Angel, *Phorlak*; King, *Ghob*

15: Now the celebrant returns in triumph unto the very centre of the circle of the arte and here they give thanks for being permitted to enter this far into the sanctuary of the Mysteries of Divinity.

Let the celebrant say:

'*Non Nobis Domine, Non Nobis*

Sed nomini tua da honouram
Propter benignitatem tuam.
Propter fide tuam'.

16: Then close with the Lesser Banishing Ritual of the Pentagram and declare the following:

'I now set free any spirits
that may have been imprisoned by this ceremony.
Go in peace to your abodes and habitations and let the
blessings of the God Most High
be about thee and upon thee now and for evermore
So Mote It Be!'

'Domine Unam Est'

The Lord is One!'

LAST WORDS

'The road goes forever on'

Throughout this book we have been working with what some occultists would call low magic. This appellation has been used to differentiate it from high magic, which is associated with such aims as self-fulfillment or mystical illumination. Low magic on the other hand is the magic of getting things done on this, the everyday levels of life.

For some, the only worthwhile goal for their magic to pursue is the higher road of illumination, but both magics have their role to play. The most important fruit of low magic is providing one with an apprenticeship for the successful practice of the higher forms of our arte, which is the raising of consciousness and the expanding of minds.

With the majority of humanity seemingly asleep to their spirituality, I am reminded of the analogy of a group of people who sit in the dark by the campfire, where they feel safe with their backs to the dark and in the comforts of the glow of the flickering fire. This is their only comfort in the cold of the night and they, in their ignorance and sloth, deny the vast dark, which is all around them and they decry any who should wander therein and know it.

But those who explore the unknown and come back, they are the knowing ones, knowing a state that the inert and the ignorant cannot comprehend. In the silence of the night, or when the firelight dims and the terror of the dark is upon them in such forms as ill health, death or disaster - what then? As they feel helpless and in the grip of an indifferent fate, they call upon a God who they think is not there and are left to wallow in the misery of their ignorance. They would have been better off to have explored, even if just a little, the great unknown.

Then and only then, will the fires burn bright, when our knowledge is increased and the shadows and the dark of our ignorance is pushed back. We, having expanded our experience, knowledge and understanding, are those who, having made the assay, have truly *'suffered in order to learn'* and subsequently can move between the worlds. Therefore the dark for us is no more.

Having had the courage and the discipline to enter therein we have robbed the dark of some of its terrors.

But even so, there are still many mysteries to explore, for the night is jealous of her secrets and our quest goes forever on.

FIAT!

Essential Reading

Whilst this work is unable to cover everything that a good occult bookshelf will hold, I suggest that you will find the following works to be invaluable. Despite the abundance of alternative publications these days there is very little good occult publishing. Indeed the highlights were the 1970's and early 19th and the 17th century, believe it or not. Particularly the 19th century copies of *The Key of Solomon* and the publishing in the 17th century of William Lilly's works on astrology, and of course the herbalist Culpeper.

William Lilly	Christian Astrology
Anthony Louis	Horary Astrology Plain & Simple
Franz Bardon	*Initiation into Hermetics, The Practice of Magical Evocation*
Samuel Mathers	The Key of Solomon, The Goetia
Israel Regardie	The Tree of Life, Ceremonial Magic
Daniel Shulkie	*Ars Philtron*
Paul Huson	Mastering Witchcraft
Lon DuQuette	My Life with the Spirits
Owen Davies	Cunning-Folk
Francis Barrett	*The Magus*

Bibliography

Agrippa, Henry Cornelius (1993). *Three Books of Occult Philosophy*, Translated by James Freake. Edited by Donald Tyson. Llewellyn.

Agrippa, Henry Cornelius (1992). *Fourth Book of Occult Philosophy*. Kessinger Publishing Company, USA.

Bardon, Franz (1962). *Initiation into Hermetics*. Kettig uber Koblenz: Osiris Verlag.

Bardon, Franz (1967). *The Practice of Magical Evocation*. Graz-Puntigam: Rudolf Pravica.

Booth, Rosemary. Unpublished Manuscript. Author's Possession.

Crowley, Aleister (1973). *777*. Weiser, Maine.

Culpeper, Nicholas (2007). *Complete Herbal*. W. Foulsham & Co Ltd, London.

Davies, Owen (2003). *Cunning Folk*. Hambledon and London.

DuQuette, Lon Milo (1999). *My Life with the Spirits*. Samuel Weiser, Maine.

Fortune, Dion (1988). *Psychic Self-Defence*. Aquarian, Wellingborough.

Howard, Michael (1977). *Candle Burning its Occult Significance*. Aquarian Press, Wellingborough.

Huson, Paul (1980). *Mastering Witchcraft*. Berkley Publishing Group, New York.

Jung, C.G. (1963). *Memories, Dreams and Reflections*. Routledge & Kegan Paul, London.

Kieckhefer, Richard (1977). *Forbidden Rites*. Sutton Publishing, Suffolk.

King, Francis & Skinner, Stephen (1981). *Techniques of High Magic*. Sphere Books, London.

Mathers, Samuel (1972). *The Key of Solomon the King*. Routledge and Kegan Paul, London

Mathers, Samuel (1997). *The Goetia*. Samuel Weiser, Maine.

Regardie, Israel (1980). *Ceremonial Magic*. Aquarian Press, Wellingborough.

Regardie, Israel (1972). *How to Make and Use Talismans*. Aquarian Press, Wellingborough.

Regardie, Israel (1978). *The Middle Pillar*. Llewellyn, Minnesota.

Regardie, Israel (1980). *The Tree of Life*. Aquarian Press, Wellingborough.

Robson, Vivian E (2001). *The Fixed Stars & Constellations in Astrology*. Ascella Publications, London.

Schulke, Daniel Alvin (2001). *Ars Philtron*. Xoanon Publishing, California.

Zalewski, Chris (1990). *Herbs in Magic and Alchemy*. Prism Press, London.

Zalewski, Pat (2000). *The Kabbalah of the Golden Dawn*. Castle Books,Victoria.

The Bible. Revised Standard Version.

Index

FOUNDATIONS OF PRACTICAL SORCERY

A seven-volume set of magical treatises, unabridged, comprising:

Vol. I - Liber Noctis

A Handbook of the Sorcerous Arte

Liber Noctis explores the attitudes, training and preparation required for success in ritual, and, as the title suggests, does not shy away from the 'darker' aspects of magic. Practical, experiential, lucid and non-judgmental, this book lays the groundwork for the successful study and practice of sorcery in the modern world.

Vol. II - Ars Salomonis

Being of that Hidden Arte of Solomon the King

Ars Salomonis is a practical manual for working with the talismanic figures found in the Key of Solomon, the most significant of all grimoires. Including two methods for empowering and activating the planetary pentacles, the author makes this vital work safely accessible to beginners. It is an ideal entranceway into the grimoire tradition.

Vol. III - Ars Geomantica

Being an account and rendition of the Arte of Geomantic Divination and Magic

Ars Geomantica explores the medieval system of Geomancy, one of the simplest and most practical of the divinatory arts. The inclusion of detailed instructions on the creation of geomantic staves, elemental fluid condensers, and talismanic construction and consecration make this work a superb introduction to an extensive assortment of magical and divinatory principles.

Vol. IV - Ars Theurgia Goetia

Being an account and rendition of the Arte and Praxis of the Conjuration of some of the Spirits of Solomon

Ars Theurgia Goetia presents a precise and practical guide to working with the spirits of this neglected text from the Solomonic grimoire cycle, the Theurgia-Goetia, giving the full seals of the spirits for the first time. The complete ritual sequence of preparation, conjuration, and license to depart is lucidly demonstrated, making this work suitable for both the beginner and the experienced practitioner.

Vol. V - Otz Chim

The Tree of Life

Otz Chim is a practical exploration of the magic of the Kabbalistic Tree of Life, the glyph that concentrates the essence of magic and mysticism within the Western Mystery Tradition. This book focuses on lesser-known aspects such as the angels associated with the paths, their seals, and invocations and includes the previously unavailable Massa Aborum Vitae.

Vol. VI - Ars Speculum

Being an Instruction on the Arte of using Mirrors and Shewstones in Magic

Ars Speculum is a concise and practical work on the use of mirrors and shewstones in magic. In it the author explores skrying and working with the four elements of air, fire, water and earth - both with elemental condensers and different elemental creatures. Other techniques include contacting other levels of being, the conjuration of spirits, binding and ligature, and healing and protection.

Vol. VII - Liber Terriblis

Being an Instruction on the seventy-two Spirits of the Goetia

Liber Terribilis is a practical study of how to work with the seventy-two spirits of the infamous seventeenth-century Grimoire, the Goetia. It also explores the vital and often neglected use of the seventy-two binding angels of the Great Name of God, the Schemhamphorasch. This volume will be of value to all levels of students and practitioners of the grimoire traditions, being based upon the work of a small group of occultists who have explored it in practice.

More information available on the Avalonia website-
www.avaloniabooks.co.uk

Or write to:
BM Avalonia
London
WC1N 3XX
England, United Kingdom

Expanding the Esoteric Horizons ...

Avalonia *is an independent publisher producing outstanding and innovative books which push the boundaries of their subjects and illuminate the spirit of the sacred in its many manifestations.*

Explore some of the other works on the occult, mythology and magic published by Avalonia at:

www.avaloniabooks.co.uk

Readers who found Foundations of Practical Sorcery of interest, is likely to enjoy:

A Collection of Magical Secrets & a Treatise of mixed Cabalah by Stephen Skinner and David Rankine

Climbing the Tree of Life by David Rankine

Living Theurgy by Jeffrey S. Kupperman

Practical Elemental Magick by Sorita d'Este and David Rankine

The Book of Gold by David Rankine & Paul Harry Barron (trans.)

The Book of Treasure Spirits, edited by David Rankine

The Complete Grimoire of Pope Honorius by David Rankine & Paul Harry Barron (trans.)

The Cunning Man's Handbook by Jim Baker

The Grimoire of Arthur Gauntlet by David Rankine

Thoth by Lesley Jackson

Thracian Magic by Georgi Mishev

Wicca Magickal Beginnings by Sorita d'Este and David Rankine

www.ingramcontent.com/pod-product-compliance
Ingram Content Group UK Ltd.
Pitfield, Milton Keynes, MK11 3LW, UK
UKHW031155080525
458350UK00001B/40